THE
ANIMAL
COURT

THE ANIMAL COURT

A POLITICAL FABLE FROM OLD JAPAN

BY JEFFREY HUNTER

TRANSLATED FROM ANDO SHOEKI'S
HOSEI MONOGATARI

NEW YORK · WEATHERHILL · TOKYO

This translation has previously appeared in *Ando Shoeki: Social and Ecological Philosopher of Eighteenth-Century Japan,* published by Weatherhill in 1992.

Illustrations are from the eighteenth-century encyclopedia *Wakan Sansai Zue.*

First edition, 1992

Published by Weatherhill, Inc.
420 Madison Avenue, 15th Floor
New York, New York 10017

Library of Congress Cataloging in Publication Data
Andō Shōeki, fl. 1744-1763. [Shizen shin'eidō
Hōsei monogatari. English] The animal court : a
political fable from old Japan / translated by Jeffery
Hunter. — 1st ed.   p.   cm.   "translated from
Ando Shoeki's Hosei monogatari ("Tales of the
world of law"), and illustrated with woodblocks of
the period"—CIP t.p. verso.   ISBN 0-8348-0268-6 :
$12.95   I. Title. B5244.A633S5413   1992
181' . 12—dc20   92-19902 CIP

ISBN 0-8348-0268-6

CONTENTS

INTRODUCTION

The Animal Court is a translation of *Hosei Monogatari* ("Tales of the World of Law") by Ando Shoeki, a largely unknown but highly original philosopher of Edo-period Japan. Shoeki was not a famous figure during his time, and what little we know about his life has been pieced together from fragments and remains fraught with uncertainties. He was born in 1703 in Niida, now Odate City in the northern Japanese prefecture of Akita. As a young man, he may have entered a Soto Zen monastery with the intention of becoming a monk. He seems to have left the Zen order for some reason and become a doctor. He probably studied in Kyoto, Japan's cultural capital, for some time, and may have visited Nagasaki and Edo. At about the age of forty, he returned to northern Japan with a wife and child to serve as a doctor in Hachinohe in what is now Aomori Prefecture. He stayed there until 1758, when he returned for unknown reasons to Niida, where he died in the tenth month of 1762.

From at least his time in Hachinohe, Shoeki began to develop his own distinct philosophy, and he also began to write it down. A circle of disciples gathered around him, men from a fairly wide variety of backgrounds and professions. An early version of his encyclopedic work *Shizen Shin Ei Do* was published, after a challenge by the censors and some strategic excisions. But after his death, Shoeki's circle broke up and his writings were lost for more than a century, when an edition of them was discovered in an antiquarian bookshop by educator and collector of rare books Kokichi Kano in 1899.

Research on Shoeki was just getting underway when the Great Tokyo Earthquake of 1923 destroyed most of the nearly complete set of his writings carefully stored at the library of the University of Tokyo. And though a few other manuscript and printed versions were later discovered, Japan's political climate from the 1920s until the end of the Pacific war was not conducive to the study of such a harsh and penetrating critic of authority as Shoeki. Only after the war did the Canadian historian E.H. Norman, working with a distinguished circle of Japanese historians, begin to open the Shoeki trunk again. Since that time, much progress has been made in the study of Shoeki, and an English translation of a selection of Shoeki's writings with a lengthy introduction by a leading Japanese scholar of the subject, Toshinobu Yasunaga, has recently been published.*

Though there is much to engage the scholar in the study of a figure as complex as Shoeki, several of his works have a much broader and more immediate appeal. *The Animal Court* is one of these works, revealing Shoeki as a parodist of Swiftian stature and an impassioned spokesman for both human and animal rights. Shoeki's prescient opinions make us think, while his wit and satire make us laugh.

SHOEKI'S WORLD

Most of *The Animal Court* is a critique of the philosophies and religions, dogmas and "isms" that reigned in Shoeki's day. They can be divided roughly into four categories. The first is the huge body of

Ando Shoeki: Ecological and Social Philosopher of Eighteenth-Century Japan (New York: Weatherhill, 1991).

Confucian literature that Japan inherited from China. Shoeki's attack starts with the mythical sage-kings of prehistory and moves through Confucius, his disciples, and all the Confucian revisionist and revivalist movements that followed over the centuries, up through and including native Japanese contributions to Confucianism.

The second target of Shoeki's criticism is Buddhism. As was true in Japan until this century, Shoeki knows little of the Indian founder of the religion or its early form in South Asia. His understanding is based entirely on traditional Japanese accounts of latter-day Buddhist sects and their doctrines, and it is the sects of Japanese Buddhism that become the particular targets of his criticism.

Shoeki also criticizes the native Japanese religion, Shinto—but since Shinto has always been a rather informal, unorganized amalgam of animistic beliefs and rituals, it isn't as easy a target as Confucianism or Buddhism.

Finally, Shoeki the doctor criticizes traditional Asian medical theory and practice with a vehemence that seems to come from personal experience. In the Asian context, his criticism of medicine is a criticism of science as a whole, for medicine in Asia played the role that physics did in Europe—it was the umbrella under which most scientific thought and experimentation took place and the language in which premodern science spoke.

Shoeki's basis for criticizing *every* "ism" in his tradition is twofold, philosophical and political. Philosophically, he claims, none of these systems apprehend the world as it truly is, and so all of them are false. Politically, they all simultaneously create and depend upon the exploitation of producers (the farmers) by consumers (the ruling elite), and so all of them are wrong.

SHOEKI'S THOUGHT

It is impossible to examine Shoeki's complex and evolving philosophy in any detail here. To fully appreciate *The Animal Court*, however, a review of a few of his major ideas is helpful.

Shoeki believed that the entire cosmos is alive, and lives by its own subtly inherent Law, which he called the Living Truth and the Way of Heaven. The world is a constant flow of the energy of the Living Truth in advancing and retreating phases.

Shoeki was an absolute dualist. Every thing and force existed, he believed, in pairs sharing mutual natures. Man and woman, for example, are such a pair, distinct as phases but essentially a dyad that only truly exists as the unit man-and-woman, or the human person. The basic unit of each form of existence is, likewise, an apparent pair of opposites that is in fact a dyad of mutual natures.

The premises of Shoeki's philosophy are rife with self-contradiction, a common feature of perennial philosophies. The edifice begins to creak and totter noticeably when he seeks to extend what was essentially an intuition—life is whole, one, and alive—and a deduction, however faulty, based on observation—that all things exist as dyads—into a cosmology that accounts for every thing and force, physical and mental, that exists. For our purposes it is enough to know that his thinking spawned a series of twos and multiples of two: two mutual natures, two phases of movement; four elements, four degrees of advancing and retreating, four parts of the body, four full organs, four empty organs; eight energies, eight organs of the face, eight emotional faculties and states, eight mental faculties and states, stars of the eight directions; sixteen periods of the year, and so on.

The linkages of these many items weaves a cat's cradle of combinations that requires more explanation than it provides, and it is ironic indeed that though Shoeki is so critical of the human proclivity for reification and grand, abstract systems of thought, he is also the originator of one more unwieldy than most, and one that, for all its claims to be based on empirical observation, is very hard to see in the life around us.

In his philosophy Shoeki allowed one major exception to the rule of twos, and in fact this is the doctrine that is most conspicuous in *The Animal Court*: the three energies, or vectors—the upward movement of energy, downward movement of energy, and sideways movement of energy. These vectors play an important role in Shoeki's view of creation by the Living Truth, and also the created: when the Living Truth moves in an upward direction, human beings are created; when it moves in a downward direction, plants are created; and when it moves in a sideways direction, animals are created.

As they are created, so are they oriented and ruled. According to Shoeki, animals, ruled by the sideways energy, are oriented sideways. They do not stand upright like human beings, their field of vision is "sideways," and they exist in a "sideways" chain of bigger eating smaller. Humans are oriented upward. They stand upright, they see forward and unobstructed, and their social order is naturally one of upright individuals, each an equal among equals.

The Way of Heaven gives to each living thing its inherently proper, right activity, which Shoeki calls Right Cultivation. The Right Cultivation of animals is to eat each other. The Right Cultivation of humankind is to cultivate grain for food and weave fiber for clothing.

This is the sum total of proper human activity, and in fact defines humanity. Anyone who fails to do so is not truly human, a point made insistently and sardonically throughout *The Animal Court*.

Thus Shoeki's natural philosophy cannot be separated from his political philosophy. While animals live in a natural hierarchy of different species, we humans are all one species. Rulers are not larger than the ruled, they don't have more eyes or hands. There is no natural form distinguishing ruler and ruled among human beings, and so those distinctions must be unnatural inventions.

Invented by whom? The sages, the Buddha, and all other thinkers and founders of religions or philosophies. And why would human beings invent such unnatural systems? The motive is greed, the desire to eat greedily without cultivating; the cause is sickness, a fluctuation in the natural upward human energy that allowed a certain individual to be born under the influence of another category of existence—the sideways-oriented animal kingdom.

SHOEKI AND ANIMALS

Following the Sino-Japanese natural history tradition, Shoeki conceived of animals divided into four types: birds, beasts (animals with fur), creatures, and fishes. We generally recognize Shoeki's birds as birds, with a few fabulous avians thrown in; beasts are mostly mammals, but not all mammals—whales are classed as fishes. The "creatures" category is perhaps the least coherent to us today, for it includes insects, most reptiles and amphibians, and even some shellfish.

Shoeki's natural history has animals created in several ways. Basically, they are products of the sideways energy in either its advancing or retreating phase, in combination with one or more of the four elements and whatever it might be linked to as a mutual nature. The energies are frequently influenced or shaped by the animal's habitat—the sea's dampness or the shade of a mountain glen. In addition, Shoeki held a theory of metamorphosis, that animals passed through stages, and just as a caterpillar changes into butterfly, a mouse grows old and turns into a bat, or a conch is a metamorphosis of a pheasant. Furthermore, in their creation or subsequent life, animals may produce "surplus energy" that becomes an "outgrowth" manifesting itself in the form of another animal—which may or may not be similar to the animal (or animals) from which the surplus energy comes. For example, the hog is said to be an outgrowth of the surplus energy of the dog and the deer.

These complicated and entirely abstract theories concerning animal origins are very strained, but Shoeki's enthusiasm for animals and his respect for their integrity as living things with their own ways and minds is heartfelt. He condescends to animals only when he forces them into human roles. When he makes them speak for themselves, it is abundantly clear that he believes they know themselves better than we do, and as such they not only deserve far better treatment than they get at the hands of humans, but our profound and humble respect as well. Their eloquent pleas to have their inherent rights respected are quite moving even today, but in Shoeki's time and culture they were positively revolutionary.

THE
ANIMAL
COURT

THE BIRDS

GATHER TO DISCUSS THE WORLD OF LAW

The birds had gathered to discuss the merits of the World of Law, and it was the pigeon who spoke first.

"Here is my considered opinion: on the land, the middle region of the earth which lies in the midst of the waters and below the heavens, a myriad of creatures flourish. Among them, human beings are dominated by the upward energy, while the sideways and downward energies inhere within them. Therefore it is that the upward flow of the Living Truth is not blocked in  humans, and their lot is to make the Right Cultivation of all the world their sole occupation, with no need to engage in other tasks. And thus it is, too, that among humankind there are no divisions into superior and inferior, noble and lowly, rich and poor. Humans do not eat humans and are not eaten by humans, they do not give or take from each other, and each finds his or her appropriate mate. This is the proper state of human society, whose essence is of the upward energy.

"We members of the animal kingdom—the birds, beasts, crawling creatures, and fish—are dominated, however, by the sideways energy, while the upward and downward energies inhere within us. Those creatures in which the advancing phase of the sideways energy is especially strong are born as birds. By nature, then, our upward energy is subdued and we are dominated by the advancing phase of the sideways energy. The Eagle, which of all birds has the strongest advancing energy, is our ruler. The Crane is our court noble, our great lord steward. The Hawk, our feudal lord; the Crow, our craftsman; the Magpie, our merchant; the Buzzard-Eagle, our master; and all the smaller birds are their servants. And so it is that the Eagle makes geese and hawks his meal, and the Hawk eats crows, sparrows, and all other birds. The Crane eats pheasants, and the Crow eats sparrows and doves. In this fashion, the larger eats the smaller. This is because we are born dominated by the advancing phase of the sideways energy, and in us the Living Truth is directed sideways. This order of eater and eaten, from large to small, is our rule and practice, the Right Cultivation as practiced by birds. We are this way because the Living Truth of Heaven runs through us in a lateral direction."

All animals are born to eat those smaller than themselves and be eaten by those larger. To eat and be eaten by each other is their original nature. But humankind is not destined to capture and eat animals. This practice was initiated by the sages, and it is a crime against nature. Here already the sages had violated the Way of Heaven.

"And you, Friend Crow, what do you think of this?"

The Crow replied. "Yes, it is just as you say. People are born with the upward energy of Heaven's Truth flowing through them, and in accord with that truth each and every one of them should make their living in the Right Cultivation of grain. Yet when the sages and the Buddha appeared in the world, they refused to cultivate the land.

First they stole the products of the Heavenly Truth of Right Cultivation and ate greedily what they did not grow; then they stole the Truth itself by inventing self-serving laws, and with the introduction of rulers, nobles and generalissimos, lords, warriors, craftsmen, and merchants, the World of Law was born. The ruler enforced the laws of the realm, and each rank on

down enforced the laws of its own station, as did those without rank or station as well. Those who violated the laws were punished with death.

"Because all, above and below, enforce and observe these laws, their world is called the World of Law. By the rule of these laws, the ruler sets the nobles and generalissimo to work for him and consumes the fruits of their labor. The nobles and generalissimo eat the fruits of the labor of the feudal lords, the feudal lords eat the fruits of the labor of their retainers, the retainers live off the labors of the craftsmen and the merchants, the master eats the labors of his servants, as do the Buddhist monks, doctors, shrine priests, and mountain ascetics. This is no different from our law of big eating small, and the human world is no different in this respect from ours. There is nothing superior or elevated about the human realm. What think you, Friend Kite?"

The Kite spoke then. "Ah, but that's not the half of it. How could we criticize the human world simply because it is no better than ours? In fact, it is worse. Among humans there are those who claim the

fields that are all part of this earthly realm and make them their kingdom, their province, their fief. They thieve the Heavenly Truth of Right Cultivation and stuff themselves greedily. And on top of that they live in a World of Law where big eats small. Yes, the human World of Law is far more deeply plunged in greed and ignorance than ours."

When the Sparrow heard these words, it hopped forward from the edge of the assembly and ventured: "It is just as Sir Kite has spoken. Humans are greedy and ignorant. But worse than that, among them is a profession called the fowler. The fowler captures us poor sparrows with bird lime and makes food of us for their hawks, and for themselves as well: roast sparrows! But we birds do not exist to be food for humans. Humans were meant to eat grains and vegetables. Now in addition to stealing the grain produced by others instead of cultivating their own, these humans kill us and eat us as delicacies! Ah, this is a great crime, surely," it cheeped, with tears plashing from its eyes.

The sight of which led the Duck, who had been sitting there all along, to raise a plaintive quack. "Yes, as the poor sparrow says, humans of the World of Law are a greatly greedy lot indeed. We ducks are birds of the water, and we live off the fishes provided us by the Truth of Heaven. There should be no reason for humans to hate us, yet they capture us with bird lime and kill us. Then they eat us, all the while claiming that we are a rare delicacy more restorative than ginseng. This is without question a great crime, and it shows that the people of the World of Law are far more steeped in sin than we poor beasts. After their deaths they are surely destined to be reborn among us and share our estate. Then their turn will come to be caught and killed by those who live in the World of Law!"

And then it was that the Pheasant strutted to the front, with his nervous little cough. "Ahem, ahem. We pheasants are born from the energy of the brush fires, we are sustained by grasses and berries, and we live according to the lot provided us by Heaven. We have never given  humans cause to hate us or made them any least trouble. Yet these humans of the World of Law, learning of our inborn shortness of breath and our inability to fly long and far (both caused, you know, by the over-strong energy of the brush fires that attend our birth), chase after us until our wind is broken and then capture us and kill us. 'Winter pheasant is delicious!' they exclaim, heaping insult on fatal injury as they devour us. The upward energy of the Truth of Heaven produced humankind and provided its right sustenance; its sideways energy produced us and gave us our proper food. Though the proper Way of each is clear, why is it that the sages, the Buddha, Prince Shotoku, and the others of the World of Law are so ignorant and greedy?[1]

"Master Snipe, do you know the reason?"

The Snipe answered. "As far as I can see, the people of the World of Law have buried deep inside themselves the upward energy that should dominate them, by reason of their being human. In its place, the sideways energy has risen to dominate them, making them no different from us. So it is that the strong and cunning ones, like the Eagle among birds, have by force made themselves rulers. Violating the Way of Heaven, they thieve the food of all beneath them and, creating the exploitative and violent World of Law, devour their ill-gotten spoils.

"Our ruler the Eagle eats all those below him in size and strength, but this is the Way of Heaven that has been ordained for us, and we who are eaten do not hate him for it. The ruler of the World of Law, however, rules without the assent of Heaven; without it, he consumes the fruits of the labors of all those beneath him. Though a human being, he is a thief far worse than any bird. And though he may be a ruler, he is no one to envy. Eventually, he will fall completely under the influence of the sideways energy and become one of us. When you realize this, it is clear that our World of Birds is superior to the human World of Law."

And just then the Black-crowned Night Heron flew in. The gathering of birds cried all together: "He has arrived! The Lesser Lord of the Fifth Rank, with his long neck and legs, his courtly robes, and a curving crown of feathers on his head!" They made him room.

After taking his seat, the Night Heron spoke. "I heard that our feudal lord the Hawk was passing, and since I would forfeit my life if I were to meet him, I was in hiding. That's why I was late. Can you please tell me what this gathering of the birds is all about?"

The Owl, in his thick-padded garment, came forward with a rustling sound. "With my reputation as a matricide, I hesitate to appear before our filial friend the Crow; allow me to screen myself,"

and he raised his silent wings about himself before opening his bill, glaring wide
with his cat's eyes, and turning to the
night heron with a recriminating hoot.[2]

"I cannot accept our friend the Night
Heron's excuse for his late arrival. He can
only be making haughty show of his rank.
At this meeting of all feathered creatures
we are debating one of the most impor-
tant issues past or present. We are discussing whether, in fact, there is
no difference between the World of Birds and the human World of
Law. There was no comparing our worlds, of course, in the age
before the appearance of the sages and the Buddha, the age when
humanity lived according to the upward energy of the Truth and all
followed the Heavenly Way of Right Cultivation. But in the ages following the appearance of the sages and the Buddha, they have
become one with us: self-serving laws were established, the Heavenly
Way of Right Cultivation was lost, and the exploitative, deceptive
World of Law was born. It is to our credit that the human world has
become like ours. You, Night Heron, grandly lift your long neck and
raise your feathery crown as you catch and eat creatures smaller than
yourself. Why, your behavior is no different from the actions of the
people of the World of Law."

The Night Heron said: "This is indeed an unprecedented debate. I
thoroughly understand that now." Just then a host of smaller birds—
the Quail, the Skylark, the Shrike, the Wren, the Siskin, the Bunting,
and the Cuckoo—came to the fore from the backmost perches and

chirped noisily in chorus. "In the World of Birds, we are those who live in the rustic villages, the poor and lowly birds. We believe that this meeting of the birds is the most important that has ever been held, and so it is we have attended in these numbers. The Crow, who is a bird of towns and villages and makes his home near humankind, is here. Why, then, is the Cock absent? Have the Crow and the Kite not noticed he has failed to attend? If he doesn't make his appearance soon, we've a mind to inform our feudal lord the Hawk and our generalissimo the Hawk-Eagle of this oversight."

Both the Crow and the Kite agreed that this was reasonable and

they selected and sent a messenger to call the Cock, upon which he made his arrival apace. "We domestic fowl are born from the energy of the heat of human homes, we live in human yards, and our sustenance is leftover scraps of human food. I simply had not heard that there was to be any meeting of the birds. I came as soon as the Crow's messenger called for me."

The Quail spoke up. "Why is it, if I may ask, that Your Honor has a crown, sports sharp spurs, and crows to greet the dawn?" The Cock replied. "My crown is a symbol of propriety, I cluck to call my hen when there is food, which shows my humanity. I have spurs to defend righteousness, and that I know the dawn shows that I have wisdom. That I never err and crow before the dawn is proof of faithfulness. In addition, I battle with every other rooster I meet, and that shows my valor. Thus I am the superior man and valiant warrior of the World of Birds.[3] The Confucian superior man of the World of

Law is a self-designated, self-made thing, but I am the true superior man, born to my rank in the World of Birds."

The Quail continued. "Ah, so there is a superior man in the World of Birds as well. Our superior man's five constant practices are far superior to those of the superior man of the World of Law, because he is born to them. Let us all pay homage to the Cock!"

And all the birds bowed low. Now the Whistling Swan was in this gathering, too, but he hadn't yet spoken a word. The Skylark faced the swan and twittered: "Swan, why do you sit there so silently?" The Whistling Swan finally spoke. "Due to my wanton ways, I have contracted venereal disease, which has risen to my head, made my face red, deformed my beak, and caused me to have a strange whistling cry. I am, you see, embarrassed to speak." But the Skylark consoled him. "I thought that only the people of the World of Law drank to dissipation and contracted venereal disease, until their bodies rotted and their noses fell off so that they wheezed like a swan when they spoke. But since in our World of Birds there are also those like your honorable self who suffer from the pox, I am confirmed in my belief that the World of Law and our world are alike."

And then the noble Crane arrived. As he alighted the other birds humbly moved aside, making room for him. The Crane trumpeted grandly: "My elongated, graceful neck and bill are my courtly robes, and my long legs that trail out behind me as I fly are my aristocratic trousers. As must be clear, I am the noble and the lord of the avian world." All the birds humbled them-

selves before the Crane with a respectful hush. The Crane continued. "I am a great minister, so I fly high and am rarely on the ground. I capture and eat the smaller creatures beneath me just as a great noble lord of the World of Law eats the labors of the officials below him. All of you: Don't think for a moment that the great nobles and court regents of the World of Birds are in any way inferior to those of the human World of Law. For here I am, in no way different from them. The sages and the Buddha made certain that there would be no differences between our world and theirs, and so it is that we are exactly alike."

The Mandarin Ducks were also present at this gathering and, with no shame before the other birds, male and female were lost in lewd caresses. The Whistling Swan, who happened to be nearby, observed aloud: "I admit it was through my own philandering that I ended up with this unseemly wheeze, but at my worst, I was never as bad as you two. Carrying on so in front of all the other birds! Have you no shame?"

The Mandarin Duck spoke up. "Look here, you've no reason to rebuke us so sharply! Why in the human World of Law, a single sage king or lord keeps many concubines, and his love play goes on in

broad daylight, sparing no one's gaze. Since those who stand at the top of human society are so, without us our World of Birds would be different from the human world, and you wouldn't want that, would you?"

The Whistling Swan relented. "I suppose we'll just have to bear it, since people seem to be imitating birds." But during this discussion, the two Mandarin Ducks were separated from each other by the enormous flock of their fellows, and the Duck, thinking that she would never find her mate again, died of heartbreak. When the Drake discovered his beloved, he spread his wings over her corpse and, consumed by grief, expired as well. The other birds looked on and lamented, "Ah, how deep was their passion!" The River Duck remarked: "But this love sickness is not limited to our Mandarin Ducks, my friends. The Buddha of the World of Law declared that the bonds of husband and wife endure into the next life. So it is that when a man and woman in the World of Law fall hopelessly in love but find obstacles in their path that prevent their marriage, they commit suicide together in hopes of meeting again in the next life. This is what happens in the human world with its Buddhist Law. All in all, it's not much different from this, is it?"

The Goose, on his ceaseless travels, had stopped in at this great congregation of the birds, and now the Magpie turned to him and asked: "You have traversed all countries and continents of the globe. Have you anything interesting to recount?"

And so the Goose reported. "Our travels span all nations and continents of the earth. That we have no settled residence is not by our own wish, but because we are moved by our natural, inherent energies and those of Heaven-and-Earth. In the winter we fly south, in the summer we fly north. In spring and fall we fly to the east or to the west. All this is in accord with the energies of Heaven-and-Earth. As a result, whatever anyone in this World of Birds wishes to know about the outside world may be learned simply by asking us.

"In the human World of Law, men build ships and sail in them to other countries, where they engage in wars. In these wars, some conquer and others are conquered. At any rate, it is for private gain alone that men travel to other countries. This is the practice of the World of Law, and an exploitative and greedy one it is. We travel from country to country to eat the different foods of each. So you see, in our World of Birds we have something not unlike men's practice of sailing from land to land. The world of humanity is no different from ours."

The Swallow was seated in a lonely corner of the group when the Shrike addressed him. "Swallow, you, too, have come from afar. Can you tell us whether your life resembles that of the human World of Law?"

The Swallow spoke: "We swallows are small birds without country or home. We wander from land to land and live in poor, borrowed quarters, under these eaves or those, never knowing the comforts of our own true home. Since only the smallest winged insects are beneath us in the hierarchy of creatures, we capture them and eat them. We know no delicacies or luxuries and live a poor life. In the human World of Law, the ruler and the feudal lords are at the top, and they enjoy a life of splendor, with all the fine foods and gor-

geous robes they could wish for. As a result, there are below them many poor, whose only home is a temporary shelter from the rain beneath a bridge, a back-street hovel, or a night's rest under borrowed eaves. There are many like these, their food and clothing rough and poor.

They are no different from we swallows in the World of Birds. This is all due to the self-serving World of Law established by the sages and the Buddha."

The Reed Warbler was perched at one side, and the Sparrow addressed him: "You, Reed Warbler, are known for your clever tongue and your sharp wit. Why do you remain so still?" And the Reed Warbler replied: "I am swift of tongue and clever of speech, and I warble about the Heavens, I twitter about the Earth, I babble about people's affairs, and I whistle a tune of all things—there is nothing I do not sing of.

"The sages, wise men, and scholars of the World of Law hold forth on the principles and phenomena of Heaven-and-Earth, humankind, and all things. They launch forth on this and that, devising systems of teachings for sale. In this way they are able to eat greedily, thieving the Way of Heaven. The Buddha, the bodhisattvas, the arhats, and the monks of every sect preach all sorts of teachings; lost in illusion themselves, they seek to lead the rest of the world there. The preachings of Confucius, the Buddha, Laozi, Zhuangzi, the doctors, and Prince Shotoku are no more than teachings that promote the selfishness, mental confusion, and reckless behavior that are the basis of the World of Law, and those teachings are no different from my ceaseless warblings.

"Before the appearance of the sages and the Buddha, the world was one of the Living Truth, Heaven's Way, and all engaged in Right Cultivation. In those days, we birds had no choice but to be humble before the world of humankind. But after the sages and the Buddha appeared, the Way of the Living Truth was lost, the artificial World of

Law was established, and humankind became the same as we. Shouldn't we rejoice, truly, that the World of Birds has grown ever more expansive with these new companions?"

And upon hearing this eloquent rhetoric, all the birds in one voice praised the Reed Warbler, proclaiming, "What a learned and brilliant fellow indeed!"

Now the great Whooper Swan was also amidst the avian assembly, and on this occasion the little Swallow turned to him and inquired: "You are majestic in size and stately in bearing, yet you do not speak. Why is this?"

Whereupon the Whooper Swan replied, "I am large and heavy and have difficulty taking flight and alighting. My immaculate white appearance is matched by a pure and undefiled spirit, free from desire. Thus is it I do not speak. In the World of Law there are men who in ignorance have a fetish about "purifying" their minds and devise all sorts of methods to accomplish this end. Bodhidharma and his monkish followers are of this ilk, just as am I, in our World of Birds."[4]

And once again the birds praised one of their number, proclaiming in unison: "The Whooper Swan is our Zen monk, the bird who has achieved Great and Total Enlightenment through his fetish with purity!"

The Cormorant was laying low toward the back of the feathered gathering when the Whooper Swan turned to address him: "Cormorant, why don't you come forward and let us know your views?" To which invitation the Cormorant replied: "You, Swan, are a waterfowl like me, but though you are heavy you float on the water's surface. I, on the other hand, ply the water's depths, catching fish that I swallow whole. Neither you nor I can survive without water. Among those of the World of Law, Laozi is the one who praises the virtues of water; and

the one who plumbs that mystical water's depths without clarifying the water's nature is none other than Zhuangzi. I, then, am the counterpart of those humans who swallow whole all their talk of the Void and the Great Way." —To which the Whooper Swan nodded his assent. Just then all the birds began to inquire where the Bush Warbler might be.

"The Bush Warbler has a lovely voice, but we haven't heard it yet. Is he here among us or has he yet to arrive?" And as they chirped and chattered thus, the Bush Warbler spoke up. "I am a small bird, born of the energy of spring's beginnings. Though I've been among you from the start, small as I am I didn't dare to add my voice to the discussion we have heard so far, the views of so many large and impressive birds. We bush warblers are born under the domination of the initial advancing energy of the element wood, produced by the Living Truth. We begin to call when the time arrives to begin Right Cultivation. We are messengers of the Way of Heaven, and our task is an important one. That is why all wait for our first calls to begin to cultivate the fields. With our lovely voices, we announce the proclamations of the True Way of Heaven to the world.

"We build our nests in precipitous places and take care not to cross the paths of larger birds. Thus it is that the sage known as Confucius of the human World of Law, envious of our virtues, commented on the ancient verse, "The warbling yellow bird / Nests high at the hillock's edge" with the words: "If a man, then, does not know his proper station, his lot is worse than a bird's." Yet even though this fellow was born a human being, it did not suit him to rest in the way of Right Cultivation; instead, he violated it, lived greedily off the labors of others who followed Heaven's Way—and he still had the nerve to envy me. He fell into the estate of the four kinds of creatures due to his own actions. All birds, hark: I, in our World of Birds, am far superior to the human sage. Indeed, I am his teacher."

The birds all gasped in surprise. The bush warbler continued. "My call was not heeded by the sages alone, but by the Buddha, too. He heard my song *'Ho, Hokecho'* ("Herald of the True Teaching") and was inspired to teach the fruits of his entire life's wisdom, the Lotus Sutra—which he called the *Hokekyo*—of the True Teaching of the Great Vehicle.[5] I was born dominated by the advancing phase of the sideways energy. It was because the Buddha was of the same nature that he was inspired by hearing my call to preach the Lotus Sutra, establishing the World of Law. On his death he was born of the sideways energy and became one of us.

"Rejoice, birds! The sages and the Buddha of the World of Law have fallen into the World of Birds and become one with us, making the World of Birds far superior to the human World of Law."

To this the gathering responded: "If that is true, our world has both Buddha and sages and is a veritable Paradise!"

The *Ran* was seated on a raised dais.[6] It's voice was gravely and thick with emotion, like that of a professional singer. The gathering of birds addressed the *Ran:* "You are a bird of a southern kingdom.

What feat or fancy are you known for?"

The *Ran* replied: "I was born in a hot land and am full of much heat energy. From birth, my voice has been throaty and tremulous. There was one of the human World of Law, in the land of Japan, who delighted in my voice. He imitated it in his own chanting of the Buddha's name and even called himself  Shinran, or "The True *Ran*." He founded the True Pure Land sect.[7] Our World of Birds, you see, provides a model for the deepest faiths of the World of Law."

The birds cried out together: "Your true name must be, then, Amida Buddha!"[8]

The Varied Tit, meanwhile, was seated in a dark corner of the assembly. The Meadow Bunting called to him: "Why don't you join the discussion?" The Tit then spoke. "I was originally a bird of a lofty mountain, but now I live on a modest hill near the capital. I forage for walnuts, and when I find one I fly high up into the heavens with it in my beak. I let it fall and hurry down again to the ground, where I wait on a rock. When the walnut hits the rock it makes a sound like a cymbal. The tapping of my beak against the walnut shell reverberates like the ringing of a temple bell. In my single-minded desire to greedily devour the walnut's sincere donation of its heart, with great concentration I peck at the shell, chanting in time 'The more the better, the more the better,' until the treat is mine. The Great Tit once challenged my faith, which prompted me to compose a written vow: 'Indeed, I am determined to get the nut's heart—the more the better!—

19

and if I don't attain my goal may I not eat the walnut and perish.' This convinced my friend of my sincerity, and he too took to tapping the walnut shell and eating its heart.

"A certain Honen, a monk of the World of Law, envied my estate.[9] Though originally a monk of a lofty mountain monastery, he came down to the capital's edge and began to spread the teachings of the Pure Land sect. He chanted the meaningless formula 'Amida, Amida' and composed his own written vow. Tapping his pilgrim's bell, he spread his faith, meanwhile greedily consuming the fruits of the labor of others. He thus became one of us. The World of Law is replete with the activities of the sideways energy."

The deadly *Chin* was perched in one of the lower seats when the Crow spied him there and called out: "*Chin,* what is it that you are known for?"[10] The *Chin* spoke up. "I eat scaleless fishes and snakes, and am myself extremely poisonous, so I hesitated to speak before this great assembly of my fellow birds. That is why I have not come forth. In the World of Law there are crafty fellows who, in imitation of my nature, are also masters of great poisons: the doctors. Though they claim theirs is the art of healing, they are ignorant of the effects of the medicines they prescribe. Their treatments are no more than the wildest guesses and their profession that of murderers. In this they learn from me. Yes, there are many of my colleagues in the World of Law."

"Indeed, indeed," nodded the feathered assembly. The *Kiba,* with its feathered form capped by two human heads, occupied a high seat.[11] The *Ran* turned to his fabulous companion and spoke: "What, *Kiba*, is your opinion of all this?" "I am a bird of myth, with one body and two heads. Thus I am a better speaker than any other bird; I have the calls of six birds altogether. In the World of Law there are monks who boast that they are masters of the six sects—the Ritsu, Kusha, Jojitsu, Hosso, Sanron, and Kegon sects.[12] But the doctrines of these six sects are all based on mistaken and unbalanced teachings dominated by the sideways energy. They were founded in envious imitation of me, with my two heads, myriad calls, and my greedy consumption of things that aren't mine. These monks who avidly devote themselves to Buddhist practices and attain enlightenment are dominated by the sideways energy and unbalanced delusions. They fall into our World of Birds and become one with us. Thus it is that the activities of the World of Law cause our World of Birds to flourish as it does."

The gathering was delighted by the *Kiba*'s speech.

All the while, the Parrot was seated to one side of the assembly. The *Chin* next turned to him and asked, "Parrot, why is it that though born a bird you mimic the speech of men?" And to this the Parrot replied: "I have a very large heart and in me the fire element is strong. The fire energy within my breast easily reverberates with the sound of human speech, and so I can imitate it. There are those like me in the World of Law. They are the Japanese monks Saicho and Kukai, who traveled to China and parroted the words of Chinese monks, transmitting to Japan the Tendai and Shingon schools—both dominated by the sideways energy and based on unbalanced delusion.[13] They themselves were first confounded and then they went on to confound the masses. They do this in imitation of me. I was born dominated by the sideways energy. The monks of the World of Law become dominated by sideways energy in their confusion about the Law and, seeking their own kind, they eventually fall into our world and become Parrots like me. Thus it is, as you can well see, that all in the World of Law wish most of all to be like us."

The Bird of Paradise was hovering over the assembly to the west, the direction from which a gentle breeze was blowing.[14] Now all the birds turned to him and said: "Please, get out of the breeze. You eat nothing but air and so you never defecate, but you fart continually. You are causing all of us great discomfort as long as you remain upwind." The Bird of Paradise was quick to reply: "I am well aware of your concern, and I do my best to stay downwind. The breeze just changed a moment ago to an eastern one, which is why I now hover in the west. As you all know, I eat nothing but air and I do nothing but fart. I have nothing at all inside me, no thing or thought; I am free of the notions of mind and self, and to me all you birds are worth less than a fart. And the fact that I am the only bird among all in the World of Birds who has attained Birdahood is attested in the scriptures: "Birdahood will never be attained by any other bird; the Bird o' Paradise is Supreme." Certain monks in the World of Law in envy imitate me with phrases like "Buddhahood will never be attained by other sects; enlightenment is limited to the Lotus Sutra." As they castigate other Buddhist sects and found their own Nichiren sect they do so in my likeness.[15]

As I see it, the entire Buddhist religion is greatly influenced by sideways energy overflowing from the World of Birds."

The Wild Dove was perched in a lowly seat. The Pigeon cooed to him: "We are of the same kind. I was the first to speak, but you have yet to say anything. Why is that?"

So the Wild Dove spoke. "I am born of the receding energy of fire, and when the corresponding season arrives I come near to human villages and call, in my country accent, 'Come out and sow, come out and sow.' For I am a messenger of the Living Truth whose role it is to announce the time for spring planting. Mine is an important part to play, as I wander from province to province, landing on a twig here and calling, landing on another twig there and making my announcement. A monk of the World of Law named Ippen chose to imitate me, calling his teaching the Ji, or "Timely" sect.[16] In their quest to greedily devour the fruits of the labor of others, the monks of this sect have been granted permission to use the government's pack horses, and they travel from post town to post town peddling holy cards proclaiming "Six Hundred Thousand Believers Born in the Pure Land," all the while ravenously consuming the donations of the faithful. Dominated by the sideways energy, and unbalanced and deluded, they join the ranks of wild doves. The Buddhism of our World of Birds is widespread even in the human World of Law!"

The Wagtail flew in just then, quite late. The other birds immediately began to ask, "Wagtail, why are you so late, in spite of the fact that you are one of the legions of the small birds?" And the Sparrow peeped up: "You have always boasted that it was you who first taught the gods Izanami and Izanagi the secret of sexual intercourse, and no doubt it was your overweening pride that quelled any qualms about arriving late.[17] But you used to be one of us, remember; you were called the Riverbed Sparrow. It won't do to be too puffed up, my friend."

The Wagtail chirped back: "You are quite mistaken. I'm not the least bit puffed up. Since I was the one who taught the two gods the method of sexual intercourse, newly fledged gods come to study with me every day and I was so busy that I simply forgot the time. Please forgive me. I became the teacher of the Izanami and Izanagi because of my suggestive habit of bobbing my head and wagging my tail. The Buddha and his monks in the World of Law now imitate me, unceasingly bobbing their heads and wagging their tails, as do the sages, the wise men, and the scholars. All of them are bobbing their heads and wagging their tails day and night, devoted to their practice of the Way of Intercourse. They are as lusty as stallions in a spring meadow. In their lewd disarray they fall under the influence of the sideways energy and are born among the Wagtails. The World of Birds will soon be throbbing to the lusty beat of their wagging bottoms."

"Yes, yes," cried all the birds, "It will soon be just as the Wagtail says, and the World of Birds will be a lively place indeed!" And they were laughing and twittering spiritedly when the Buzzard-Eagle came flying and shrieking his high-pitched, metallic call, *"Heee, heee."* The gathering of birds was startled and crouched in fear as the Buzzard-Eagle landed on the branch of a tree a little above them and proclaimed: "Hear ye, birds. I am the footsoldier of the World of Birds, and my legions are great. If any of you commit an offense I report it to the chief retainer of the feudal lord, the Peregrine Falcon. Depending upon his judgment, you may be captured, torn to bits, and eaten. This I warn you in advance."

Then the Falcon arrived with a great following. They perched in a slightly taller tree and the Falcon looked down on the Buzzard-Eagle and spoke. "Have you made my proclamation known to all the birds?"

The Buzzard-Eagle hunched down and replied. "I have made it known just as you commanded."

The Peregrine Falcon turned to the assembled birds. "Listen well, birds. I am the chief retainer of the Hawk, who is the feudal lord of our World of Birds. Remember me well."

And all the birds crouched low in fear. Just then the lesser birds that served as forerunners for the Hawk began to arrive and announced to the Falcon: "The Hawk is on his way!"

The gathering of birds crouched even lower and the Hawk arrived, settling on the branch of a tall tree. He addressed the Falcon. "Chief Retainer Falcon, have you made clear my will to all the birds?"

"I have made it known just as you com-  manded," replied the Falcon. "I," said the Hawk, "am the feudal lord of the World of Birds. Remember me well." And he opened his large eyes and glared at them. The smaller birds shivered with fear and felt as if they were to be torn to bits on the spot. As they crouched even lower, there was a mighty rushing of wings as the

Hawk-Eagle, accompanied by a large following, alighted on the peak of a small boulder facing the gathering. The Hawk bent low before him, and the Hawk-Eagle let out a great screeching *"Hyuuu"* and began to speak. "I am the generalissimo of the World of Birds, and I grasp that world in my talons. It is within my power to catch and eat any of you, from Hawk on down to the multitude of smaller birds, and I will not brook any laxity on your parts. Birds, the generalissimo of your world is none other than I. Know this well." And as he glared at them, his eyes glinting with wrath, the multitude of birds was half-dead with fear.

They remained pressed to the earth when the regal swooshing of the Eagle's wings were heard. He arrived with a large following and the sound of their flight caused the birds to gasp and press even closer to the earth. The Eagle and his retinue perched on the tip of a great crag opposite the gathering, and the Eagle let out a mighty cry. Then he began to speak in majestic tones. "I am the ruler of the World of Birds, the unsurpassed Lord Eagle (for the Phoenix is a bird of India). All of you, from the Crane, the Hawk-Eagle, the Hawk, the Falcon, the Buzzard-Eagle, and the multitude of small birds on down, are my possessions. Any who disobey my orders will be immediately captured and torn to bits. All you birds, obey my commands."

And the Eagle continued. "The order of large and small, strong and weak in the World of Birds is the doing of the Truth of Heaven. Our world is created when the Truth of Heaven circulates as sideways energy. The human world was created when the Truth of Heaven circulated as upward energy and all were originally engaged in Right Cultivation. Then, there were no distinctions between superior and inferior, large and small, high and low. All were created equal, without distinction. Yet from the time of the appearance of the sages and the Buddha, self-serving laws were established and the human world has modeled itself upon our World of Birds. In imitation of me, the Eagle, the ruler was created; in imitation of the Hawk-Eagle, the generalissimo was

created; in imitation of the Crane, the nobility were created; in imitation of the Hawk, the feudal lords were created; in imitation of the Falcon, the senior retainers, stewards, and other officials were created; in imitation of the Buzzard-Eagle, the footsoldiers were created; in imitation of the multitudes of lesser birds, the four classes of commoners were created; in imitation of the Wagtail, the diviners and mountain ascetics were created; in imitation of the *Chin,* the doctors were created; in imitation of the Whooper Swan, the temple priests were created; in imitation of the Cormorant, Laozi and Zhuangzi were created; in imitation of the Wren and the Bunting, the beggars and outcasts were created. In this fashion, the human World of Law was created in imitation of the World of Birds."

There are great similarities between the human World of Law and the World of Birds. In the World of Birds, the rule provided by Heaven is that larger eats smaller. But when a buzzard-eagle is, first, caught and kept by humans and, later, released and allowed to return to the wild, it can no longer catch the smaller birds it once lived on. Instead, it flies wildly about trying to escape them and in the end dies of starvation. In the World of Law, the footsoldier shares this fate. When he is deprived of his stipend, he becomes a beggar or an outcast, he is forced to cringe before the merchants and farmers that he formerly plundered, and he suffers greatly. A falcon or hawk captured and kept by men, when returned to the wild, is attacked and pecked to death by the crows that it once preyed on. Those of the same rank in the World of Law share the same fate. When the senior retainers, officials, or feudal lords are defeated in battle, they flee for their lives and are forced to cringe before the merchants and farmers that they once preyed upon. Even a hawk-eagle captured and kept by men, when returned to the mountains from which it came, is set upon by the swans and geese that it once preyed on and chased about until it finally weakens and dies. In the same way, when the generalissimo of the human World of Law is defeated in battle during an uprising, he becomes an outcast who must cringe before the peasants and live off their favors until he is finally discovered by his enemies and killed. An eagle, too, caught and kept by men loses its strength and, when returned to the mountain fastnesses, is no longer able to capture the night herons and geese that were once his prey. In the end he weakens and dies. The ruler of the human World of Law shares the eagle's fate. When, in an uprising, he is defeated in battle, he is forced to flee and hide in a farmer's home, until he is finally sought out by his enemies, captured, and killed. This is a great similarity between the human World of Law and the World of Birds. Since birds are dominated by the sideways energy according to Heaven's plan, this is not their failing. But humans are born dominated by the upward energy, and the way provided to them is that of Right Cultivation by each and every person. When they fall under the influence of one-sided beliefs and sideways thinking, falling to the same level as the World of Birds, this is a great and serious failing—it's extent "inexpressible in words, utterly beyond the mind's grasp."[18] All the Confucian writings and classics from the time of Fuxi to Confucius are just poor imitations of the twittering of the reed warbler and the mindless repetitions of the parrot.[19] The teachings of Master Cheng are imitations of the shrike,[20] and Zhu Xi's teachings are modeled after the skylark's trillings.[21] The wren's chirps were the pattern for Sorai's teachings,[22] and the piping of the quail laid the plan for the literary studies of the Tang, Song, and Ming dynasties. All literary studies and criticism are nothing but the peeping of birds. Japanese poetry is in imitation of the little cuckoo's song, and Noh chants are modeled after the siskin's call. Rites and music are in imitation of the bunting's notes. The chanting of the puppet theater copies the cry of the snipe. In imitation of the kingfisher's plaintive call, men pluck the samisen, koto, and zither while, following the mandarin duck's lead, they lose their heads in lust and drink. The pheasants, in fear of the eagle and the hawk-eagle, hide in the holes of trees and fight among themselves for food; imitating their behavior, men take to gambling, and gambling leads to arson and thievery. Thus it is that every activity of the human World of Law finds it model in the World of Birds.

Now one might well ask why it is that humans should want to imitate birds, particularly in the matter of government. And to this I would reply: People are not aware of the fact that they are imitating the World of Birds. Birds are born dominated by the sideways energy and humans are born dominated by the upward energy, thus they are inherently different. But when people grow dominated by the one-sided notion of "purity," when their minds grow unbalanced and prejudiced, the upward energies are blocked, they become dominated by the sideways energy, and they proceed to create the World of Law. The law itself is an expression of the sideways energy. Law could never be created as long as the upward energy dominates, for upward energy moves with great speed, always in accord with Heaven's movements; it never moves in a lateral direction. The domination of the sideways energy results when the upward energy is blocked and redirected to one side, when it can no longer penetrate directly. Thus it is that those dominated by the sideways energy do not realize their predicament and establish laws, and all that passes in the World of Law is the activity of the sideways energy. This is why human beings, though they are not aware of it, have become no different from the birds. Birds that have been captured by people and kept in cages cannot proceed through the stages of their life cycle as they would in their natural habitat, and so they die. And birds that have been kept in captivity for a long time are no longer able to survive when returned to the wild, for in their long contact with the upward energies of their human keepers they lose their own sideways energy as birds. Unable to adapt to the sideways energy of their original wild environment, they die. Among wild birds, one in five or six hundred is a human being [who has been reborn as a bird]; and even if its parents should try to raise it on grain, the natural food of humans, it dies, because it's human, upward energy is suffocated by the sideways energy of birds. In its normal, erect posture, a bird's field of vision is mainly lateral, since its eyes are on the sides of its head, and its vision is limited. It cannot see in an unobstructed manner from top to bottom. This is because it is dominated by the sideways energy. The sages and the Buddha looked at the world in an artificial manner and their field of vision was broad laterally, but muddled and unclear. That is why they saw fit to establish laws, preach many different kinds of sermons, and indulge in many different practices. They did not know that when we are able to see clearly from top to bottom, without any obstructions, when our minds and our wisdom are direct and straightforward, there is no need to establish laws of any kind, and they could not know this because they themselves were under the domination of sideways minds. This all resulted in the human World of Law coming to resemble the World of the Birds so remarkably.

The birds then all cried in one voice: "Though the World of Law and the World of Birds are nearly identical, there is one difference. Birds cannot capture people. Nor do birds catch other birds and put them in cages. People, on the other hand, capture the larger birds of prey and keep them in hawkeries, further capturing smaller birds to feed to them; they also net small birds and put them in cages, to enjoy the beauties of their songs. These deeds are certainly far beyond the scope of the sideways energy of birds!"

"Yes, many people capture my kind!" said the Bush Warbler. "Recently, more and more people have been capturing us, too," piped the Quail. The Black-faced Bunting added, "There are bird dealers who keep millions of our kind in their shops and sell us for a living. This sort, in addition to being strongly possessed by the sideways energy, are great criminals, deeply steeped in evil. They will plummet quickly to our world. What can they be thinking that they fail to understand how it would feel if they were put in a cage, if their wife and children were put in cages, and taken to be sold! No, they do not deserve to be regarded as human beings."

And now the birds delivered their final judgment.

"Is there any bird in this assembly who suffered a famine or a year of poor harvest? Is there any bird who has been reduced to grinding poverty because he could not repay a loan? Any bird who has suffered because harvest and land taxes were extorted from him? Any bird who, under the provisions of the tax-collecting law, robs another of its food? Any bird who levies "special contributions" and "donations" from others? Is there any bird who makes great show of his wealth by acting the grand patron? Is there any bird who, winning a battle or a war, becomes our Emperor Eagle? Or can our Emperor Eagle, by losing a battle or war, fall to the estate of outcast? Let all consider these facts."

And so it was that they concluded: "All these troubles and confusions are part of the World of Law of human beings. In our World of Birds, these things do not exist, nor can any one of us, reduced to poverty, be forced to sell our very home. Considering all this, the World of Birds is far superior to the human World of Law. In comparison, ours is a paradise, a realm of great peace."

Since there is neither silver nor gold in the World of the Birds, there is neither greed nor delusion, thievery nor war.

THE BEASTS

GATHER TO DISCUSS THE WORLD OF LAW

The domestic beasts and beasts of human settlements, beasts of the fields and beasts of the mountains, beasts of the rivers and beasts of the sea, all without exception gathered to discuss the human World of Law.

The Horse began. "We horses are born from the energy of the fires of human homes. In the world of Heaven's Truth, we were meant to help mankind by carrying fertilizer on our backs, by pulling the plow, and in general assisting the True Man in his Right Cultivation. We work in accord

with the lot provided us by Heaven, and in return humans care for us and we are able to preserve our lineage from generation to generation. All beasts are born dominated by the retreating phase of the sideways energy. For that reason all can run, but none can fly. We are covered with fur, not feathers, and in this all beasts are alike.

"After the appearance in the world of the sages and the Buddha, however, who with natures dominated by the sideways energy established the World of Law, the equestrian art was born. Men put steel bits in our mouths and stuck hot peppers into our anuses, they cut and trimmed our hooves and branded our hides, they rode us to exhaustion and refused to allow us to eat as we liked. These were sufferings hard to bear. In their world footsoldiers were treated as badly as we and tortured in the same ways. Why, sometimes they were forced to run thirty leagues in a single day! This pace puts even our swift legs to shame. It is because of the World of Law that these foot-soldiers, though born as human beings, must do the work of horses.

"Then, too, humans set fifty or a hundred mares loose in a pasture and introduce a single stallion to mate with them all. They do this to beget fine young colts. In imitation of this, the ancient emperor Shun kept in addition to his wife many concubines and ladies-in-waiting, mating with them all—and in broad daylight, too.[23] He did this in order to beget fine young sages. Though born a human being, Shun's behavior was that of a wild horse. The human world based on Heaven's Truth is one of Right Cultivation for all, with all their energies. Man and woman, husband and wife, are a unit, and no man should mate with any other woman, no woman have intercourse with any other man. The coupling of True Men and Women should be like the coupling of the spirits of Heaven and Earth, the Sun and the Moon, and that is how True Children are begotten. The hearts and minds of the sages and the Buddha are dominated by a tendency toward the sideways energy, and so they established sideways laws and created the World of Law. It is due to this World of Law that human beings behave like untamed horses."

In the hierarchy of beasts, the *Doku* is the emperor[24], the Elephant the aristocrat, the Lion the generalissimo, the Tiger the feudal lord, the Ape is the senior retainer and adviser, the Bear is the retainer, the Wolf the warrior, and the Horse the footsoldier. The lesser animals—the Deer, Wild Boar, Hog, Fox, Raccoon-Dog, Badger, *Kusai,* Monkey, Rabbit, Ox, Dog, Cat, Mouse, Weasel, and the rest—are the craftsmen, the merchants, the monks, the Shinto priests, the mountain ascetics, the doctors, the beggars, and what remains of society. All are governed by the principle that larger devours smaller.

The Ox was in a lower seat, peacefully chewing its cud, when the *Doku* addressed him: "You, Ox, are a domestic beast. Why do you hesitate to give your opinion?"

The Ox replied. "We Oxen are born of the energy of the water used in human homes. We carry heavy burdens, plow the fields, and assist with Right Cultivation. This is our purpose. But since the advent of the World of Law, humankind has taken to butchering us. They devour

our flesh for their own nourishment; they flay us and press elixirs from our hides, then tan them for leather; they make tallow from our fat; and they extract our gall stones for medicine. How they make us suffer! Every day they butcher hundreds of thousands of our kind. They even kill us as sacrificial offerings to Heaven! How could Heaven be pleased at this?

"In the World of Law, the day and hourly laborers are forced to bear heavy burdens; sweat as thick as glue or oil pours down their backs and they suffer as if flayed. They die without ever having known a moment's ease. These humans share our Oxen's fate."

The Dog was seated outside the assembly. The Raccoon-Dog spoke up: "When you, Sir Dog, spot any other beast, you're immediately off and yapping, trying to catch and eat it. It's not like you to sit so still."

The Dog replied: "We Dogs are born of the energy of the pots and pans of human homes. We eat leftover scraps of human food and uneaten rice. We help our masters by barking at suspicious shadows and thieves. We do not cultivate but greedily devour our masters' leftovers because we are born dominated by the sideways energy. Since this is the role provided us by Heaven's Truth, it is not our failing. But many in the World of Law are our imitators: the Confucian scholars and sages from generation to generation, age to age, including Fuxi, Shennong, Huang Di, Yao, Shun, Yu, Tang, Wen, Wu, the Duke of Zhou, Confucius, Zisi, Mencius, Zhouzi, Chengzi, Zhuzi, and the scholars of the Tang, Song, Ming, and before that, Han dynasties[25]; the many Zen patriarchs and Buddhist scholar-monks through the ages since the time of Shakyamuni; the Taoists Laozi, Zhuangzi, Liezi, and Huainan[26]; in Japan, Prince Shotoku and the generations of scholars, on up to Hayashi Razan and Ogyu Sorai. All of them appropriate the fruits of the labors of the many, produced in accord with Heaven's Way, without engaging in cultivation themselves. They greedily devour the leftovers of the many, yet they know nothing of the Subtle Way of mutual natures. They were born of unbalanced energies, and they gather the suspicious shadows of their unbalanced feelings and unbalanced thoughts into books. They create words and writings as tools to thieve Heaven's Way, and with them they record and read suspicious shadows. None of the countless passages in books tells of the Way of Heaven's Truth; each is nothing more than arbitrary and willful falsehood. Compared to the Subtle Way of the Living Truth—which through its own activity, in advancing and retreating phases, produces the eight energies that in turn, in their mutual relationships and through the circulation of the upward, downward, and sideways energies, produce Heaven-and-Earth, humanity, and all things, each completely provided with the Subtle

Way—compared to that, the teachings that are regarded as the basics of all learning, that is, divination, astrology, the five constant practices, the five virtues, the Buddhist doctrines such as "the unborn and the undying"—all of these are nothing more than the products of a mind misled by unbalanced intellect. They are no more than shadows of the Subtle Living Truth which unfolds as mutual natures. The teachings of Confucianism, the preachings of the Buddha, the writings of Laozi and Zhuangzi, the medical treatises, the Shinto texts, and in addition all poetry and literature are nothing more than the yapping of a dog at an insubstantial shadow. But barking at shadows is actually the task of us dogs. These men of the World of Law, the sages and Shakyamuni, the teachers and the monks and all scholars and literati, are of our ilk—we who, dominated by the sideways energy, are fated to howl at mere shadows. They are so like us even in life that there can be no doubt that upon their deaths, according to the laws of metamorphoses, they will fall into birth among the beasts.

"Though I am but a dog, in the World of Beasts I am the Sage, the Buddha, the Confucian Ruler, the Buddhist Patriarch. All of you must pay me homage." And the beasts assented to this.

Only the Monkey, whose hate for the Dog was an ancient one, took exception. But the Dog spoke to him directly: "There is no reason for you to hate me. The sages and great teachers, Shakyamuni and the learned Patriarchs of the World of Law, defame those who disobey the laws as 'dogs,' revealing only how blind they are to their own condition, which is truly that of dogs! It applies more to them than any others.

There is also the popular saying, 'Monks and samurai are scavenging dogs.' Shakyamuni is the ancestor of all monks, and the samurai are the descendants of the Confucian Ruler and the sages. This expression means that the sages, Shakyamuni, and dogs are all completely alike. How true this is indeed! We dogs do not cultivate, but live off other's food. The sages do not cultivate, but greedily devour the Right Cultivation of others. The Buddha did not cultivate, but greedily devoured the offerings of others. With their teachings, their lectures and preachings, they howl at the shadow of the True and Subtle Way. We dogs, too, yap at shadows. Thus it is that we are not the tiniest bit different in heart, in mind, in behavior, or in deeds. Since it is the Living Truth residing within the people of the world that recognizes this fact and makes the people create the saying 'Monks and samurai are scavenging dogs,' how can it be denied? I may be a Dog, but the sages and the Buddha are my peers. That is why they say, 'Even a puppy possesses the Buddha nature.' "[27]

And all the beasts paid their respects to the Dog.

The Cat was in a corner of the assembly. The Fox turned to her and asked, "Why do you remain so still?" And the Cat spoke up. "When I dance with you, you sing as I play the flute.[28] In imitation of us, the people of the World of Law perform music and the Noh drama. Now my kind is born from the energy of the hearth ash of human homes, and the lot provided us by Heaven is to catch and eat mice. Mice only come out at night. Accordingly, Heaven's Truth has given me eyes that can see in the dark. My pupils have four phases, from the thinnest slit to seed-shaped to oval to round. These wax and wane in accord with the eight divisions of the day and night. Since I was born of the energy of ash and ash is earth, and since earth has the Subtle Function of controlling the changes in the four elements, that ability has also been given to me, and I can control the changes in my pupils so that I can see in the dark and catch and eat mice.

"But I grow lazy in my hunting and, leaving my master's house, wander and stray here and there, stealing food. There are people in the World of Law who imitate me, never staying at home but rushing about to other's homes, neglecting their own work until finally they are reduced to poverty. These ones are of my ilk."

The Mouse was hiding in a hole in the ground, terrified to be in the same assembly with the fearful Cat. The Weasel reassured him: "Mouse, you need not fear the Cat. This is a general assembly of all the beasts. And while it is true, as was concluded in the assembly of the birds earlier, that the human World of Law is no different from our World of Beasts, and large eats smaller and smaller eats smaller still, during this assembly we are all equals. There is no need for the large animals to fear each other, and it is also forbidden for the larger animals to catch and eat the smaller. So take heart, and let us know what you think."

And the Mouse spoke. "I am born of the energy of the smoke of human dwellings, and just as there is nothing in their homes that smoke does not permeate, including their furnishings, their clothing, and their food, there is nothing in human homes that is not my proper fare. Why, Heaven

has provided me with the task of eating even the fleas on my own back. My fear of the Cat prevents me from appearing during the day, and I only come out at night. In homes where a cat's not about, I set to chewing on whatever food I may find at hand.

"Among those of the World of Law, there are no end of people who do not cultivate but fancy fine food and clothes; rulers who out of love of luxury oppress their subjects below; those who, in imitation of their rulers, thieve Heaven's Way; and those who imitate me by creeping out at night, sneaking into other's homes, and stealing their property. All of these are my fellows, and thus it is that there is no difference between the World of Law and the World of Beasts. That is the reason, in fact, that the words for mouse and thief are similar in sound."[29]

The Bat was perched, hanging upside down, on the withered branch of a tree at the front of the assembly. The Ape addres-sed him: "It is unseemly for you to hang from that tall tree on the occasion of this momentous assembly. Come down from your perch!"

The Bat descended from his perch and bowed before the assembly. "I am an aged transformation of a Mouse. I eat mosquitoes and breathe smoke. Attached to my body are these flaps that resemble wings but are not wings. Nevertheless, I can fly with them. My form resembles a beast's but is not a beast's. I resemble a bird but am not a bird. Mine is a strange shape, on the boundary between birds and beasts.

"In imitation of me, all the Buddhist monks of the World of Law—

those of the Ritsu, Kusha, Jojitsu, Hosso, Sanron, Kegon, Tendai, Shingon, Pure Land, Ikko, Lotus, Zen, and Ji sects—starting with Shakyamuni himself, all wear long-sleeved robes that resemble a bat's wings but are not a bat's wings. Their hearts are distorted by confusion, their minds deluded with desires and truly beastlike, but their form is human, not bestial. Theirs is a strange shape, on the boundary between humans and beasts, which puts them in my company. Thus it is that though I am a small animal, I am the Buddhist monk of the World of Beasts. All beasts, bow before me!"

The Weasel came forward, squeaking as it did so, "I am born of the smoke of human homes that collects beneath the verandah or between the logs in the woodpile. I catch and eat mice. I also eat insects. When I chance upon a piece of fish destined for the human table, I drag it off and store it away. I like to eat things a little bit at a time. There are in the World of Law people who imitate me. They save up great stores of foodstuffs, and even though it's rotting they refuse to offer it to others; nor can they eat that much themselves at one sitting."

From a hole in the loose earth at the side of the gathering the Mole stuck out his head and said in a whisper: "I am born from smoke that collects in loose earth, and since the advancing phase in me is very weak, I die at once if I'm exposed to the sun's rays. Let me speak my piece from here. In the World of Law there are those who like me hate the sun and never go out of their houses. Without cultivating, they eat greedily. And

should they chance to go outside and be exposed to the sun, the wind, or the rain, they lose their bearings, sicken, and die. These ones are like me."

The Raccoon-Dog sat hunched in the assembly feigning sleep. The Ape reproached him, "Raccoon-Dog, that's an old, old trick of yours. Stop pretending to be asleep and tell us what you think." With some embarrassment, the Raccoon-Dog spoke up. "I am born of the fire energy as it collects in holes in hills. I am a beast because I am so strongly influenced by the retreating phase of the sideways energy. I eat fieldmice and fruits and seeds. I can't sleep because I am so full of the fire energy. And so in an attempt to actually sleep I feign the act. People may well spy me in this pretended sleep and, planning to kill me, approach closely. At times like this, because I have too much fire energy, I fart. My farts are very strong smelling, so strong that the people gasp and squint and end up losing all sense of where they are. I enjoy confounding people like this. There are people in the World of Law who imitate me by putting on a sleepy face when all the while they are cleverly scheming to deceive others, to greedily acquire things, and to borrow money from others with no intention of repaying it. These ones are of my ilk."

The Badger was crouched in a small hollow of the assembly, glaring at the Dog, because he was frightened of it. The Dog inquired, "Why do you glare at me so?" To which the Badger replied, "I am an aged transformation of the Raccoon-Dog, and I am extremely weak. When I look at you and see how strong you are, I am terrified that you will do me in in one bite. That is why I do not take my eyes off of you. I am too full of the retreating phase of the fire energy and the warm, moist energy, so that when I feel the presence of human beings I always fart. When people smell my fart, their eyes grow dim and they mistake me for another human being. I entertain myself by deceiving people in this way.[30] There are those of the World of Law who imitate me. With jabber as mindless as my farts and all sorts of confusing behavior they darken people's eyes and confuse their minds with the purpose of appropriating or stealing their goods. They don't commit grand thefts, but they are good at little capers. These clever thieves are of my ilk."

The Fox was pressed to the ground in a corner of the gathering because he, too, was fearful of the Dog. The Cat turned to the Fox and addressed him: "My friend, why not speak up?" The Fox began. "I am born of the energy of brush fires, I live in the fields and eat fieldmice and snails. I dig a hole in the earth of the fields and make it my den. Since I am born with too much of the hot, damp fire energy, a foul odor clings to me. My breath and my farts are strong smelling. The energy of brushfires clings to my tail, and when that energy comes into contact with the dark night air, my tail seems to burn like a torch. When a person approaches me and comes into contact with my foul-smelling breath, he is suddenly taken ill, is frightened, and grows confused and disoriented. The path I am traveling appears to him to be a road, and he follows after me. I take advantage of his confusion and approach. If he has food with him, I snatch it and devour it. If not, I abandon him there and disappear.[31]

"Strong as the energy of brushfires is in me, my body and mind are full of the sideways energy and I am extremely wary. But this is

my nature by birth, and no fault of mine. Yet there are people in the World of Law who, though born dominated by the upward energy, lost themselves to desire and fell under the sway of the sideways energy. Without cultivating, they thieved Heaven's Way, devoured it greedily, and for their own selfish purposes created self-serving laws and established the World of Law. These humans, who are of the upward energy by nature, have given themselves to the sideways energy; in other words, these people have changed into foxes! Such people of the World of Law who are full of desires and extremely wary are of my ilk. The people of the World of Law point at me and say that foxes transform themselves into human beings, but this is a delusion caused by the sideways energy. I do not change into a human; human beings transform *themselves* into foxes!

"Because people are deluded by the influence of the sideways energy they grow extremely wary, and their emotions and their intellects are crazed. Their delusions take myriad forms. There are the teachings of Confucianism, from divination, astrology, the zodiac, the five elements, the five virtues, and the four social classes[32] to the teaching of the gap between the ordinary human heart and the heart committed to the Way, which is the Impartial Way to be taken.[33] There are the myriad Buddhist teachings, from the Buddha mind, the mind of sentient beings, the unborn and the undying, the five periods, and the Right Teachings, to realizing enlightenment, Right Enlightenment, and the One Come From Enlightenment.[34] There are the Taoist teachings of attaining immortality and the action of nonaction. There are the instructions of the military leaders, their strategies and battle methods. There are the teachings of the doctors, the twelve meridians and medicines created in ignorance of the true flow of the vital energies.[35] There are the Shinto teachings of the seven generations of heavenly deities and five generations of earthly deities. There are literary studies, such as the *Classic of Rhymes,* which teaches the proper rhymes in Chinese poetry, or works that teach the methods of composing Japanese poetry. All of these writings and all of this learning thieve Heaven's Way and are delusions of the sideways energy. Their pursuit leads to birth in the four realms, as a Fox. So it is that I am the most learned one of the World of Beasts, and all scholars of the World of Law are my students."

The Marten was rushing about restlessly at the edge of the assembly, unable to keep still in a seat. The Badger was irked by his pacing and called to him, "You, Marten, it's rude of you to be scampering about here and there instead of keeping your seat in this great assembly. Sit down and speak up." The Marten began: "I am born of the weak energy of the warm dampness of the hills and fields. I eat the insects that trill in autumn and make my den in a hollow tree. My coat is soft and warm. I gladly greet the cold weather, but suffer when it's hot. Since I am full of damp warmth, my mind is sullied and I am foolish and rather dull.

"In the World of Law there are those who imitate me and rush madly about, hating to stay at home. They are inattentive and neglect their livelihoods, and they are unable to properly support themselves. These ones are of my ilk."

The Rabbit lay crouched in the assembly's midst, with his long ears perked and his restlessly wandering gaze. He came forward to

say: "I was born of the energy of the clear Moon. I prefer to be near water, for I value its softness and the virtue of clarity that resides within it. My main food is the bark of trees. I was born of the water energy of the Moon, and water's mutual energy, wood energy, inheres within me. As a result, my forelegs are short (in accord with the water and wood energies) and my hind legs are long (in accord with the fire and metal energies). Since the water energy rules the night, so I, in harmony with the water energy of the Moon, can transform myself into a shadow, and like the moon I disappear and appear again with ease.

"There are in the World of Law those who imitate me, and proclaim that water is 'the mystery of mysteries.' They value water's softness, and the fact that it does not resist. Lost in their admiration for it, they make it their ultimate truth. One of these [Laozi] taught that immortality could be achieved by nourishing the spirit, and he transformed himself into a genie who could fly through the air; another [Zhuangzi] worshiped his example, and retreated to "the village of non-being"; yet another [Liezi] learned to ride the wind, and he declared that the cosmos began in primordial chaos. All of these were drowned in the water they so worshiped and they fell into the sideways energy, becoming members of my tribe. I, you see, am the Taoist of the World of Beasts."

The Ape was at one side of the assembly, first hiding and then leaping out, never sitting still. The Fox addressed him: "Ape, how unseemly your darting about is! Why do you leap in and out of hid-

ing in this great and majestic assembly?"
The Ape replied. "I am an aged transformation of the Marten. When his stupidity
waxes to its epitome, he is transformed
into an Ape. That is why I am so wary and
am always hiding, then appearing again,
always restless, never still. When I

encounter humans, I rush up into the trees. When they leave, I
descend. I climb up again and descend again, unable to make up my
mind. That is why when the ones in the World of Law who imitate
me created the grammar of classical composition—which is the tool
they use to thieve Heaven's Way—they used the Chinese character for
'ape' as a marker to send the reader up and down the sentence, forc-
ing him to read the character twice.[36] They regard the grammar of
sentences as the very foundation of learning. They do not know that
grammar is in fact a great sin born of an intelligence deluded and
warped by the sideways energy, that it results in greedily devouring
Heaven's Way without cultivating, and so they fall into the four
realms quick as a wink. These grammarians are of my ilk. I am the
literati of the World of Beasts."

The River Otter was at the back of the gathering and, after listen-

ing to everyone's remarks, he came forward
himself. "I am an aged transformation of
the Cat. I live in rivers, where I catch and
eat fish. When I grow even older I become
a water sprite and make my home in
rivers close to human habitations.[37] When
someone falls into the river I pull them to

the bottom and rip out their bowels, which I eat. After I have eaten the bowels of a human being, I am able to take on human shape, a trick I use to seduce prostitutes and to raid farmers' fields, making off with the vegetables I like to eat.

"There are those in the World of Law who imitate me by adopting false guises and seducing the wives of other men and losing themselves to love play until they finally meet their proper punishment, forfeiting their lives for their pleasures. These ones are of my ilk. I am the philanderer of the World of Beasts."

The Seal was in a far seat when the Cat addressed him. "You are a beast of the sea, and have come from afar to join us. You deserve a warm welcome for your pains."

The Seal replied: "I am born when the metal energy, which shares mutual natures with the retreating fire energy of the salt in sea water, blended with the damp energy, circulates in a sideways direction. I am wrapped in warm energy, and my body temperature is high. I live off fish that I catch, and when the sun shines I float and frisk on the waves, where I also take my rest.

"Those who are doctors in the World of Law practice their profession in imitation of me. They try to settle their patients' stomachs with warm things. And, believing that increasing the strength of the kidneys is the most important thing for preserving health, they regard Seals born in China and grown to maturity in the northern seas as a precious medicine. Yet they know nothing of the circulation of the energies of the seas of China or the northern land of Ezo [Hokkaido].

They do not know that the vital spirit of humans is to be found in grain, not in the fluids of the liver. They delude the people of the world with their arguments based on the foolish supposition that the vital spirit of the liver should be recklessly strengthened. They may even kill their patients, without the least understanding of their error. In their ignorance they are no different from me, who was born in the seas of Japan and knows nothing of the flow of energies in China. The doctors of the world are all of my ilk. I am the doctor of the World of Beasts, and the doctors are the Seals of the World of Law."

The Hog, big and fat, was in the gathering, and he grunted his assent before speaking up in a slow, thick, round, voice. "I was born from the surplus energy of the Dog, but there is much damp energy in me, I am fat, and my movements are slow. Though I resemble a dog, I am not a dog. My motions resemble a deer's, but I am not a deer. I stand between the Dog and the Deer.

"There are people like me in the World of Law. They offer prayers, so they resemble Shinto priests, but they are not Shinto priests. They recite the sutras, so they resemble Buddhist monks, but they are not Buddhist monks. They stand between Shinto priests and Buddhist monks, these mountain ascetics. These ones are of my ilk. I am the mountain ascetic of the World of Beasts, and the mountain ascetics are the Hogs of the World of Law."

The Deer stepped forward, shaking his antlers. "I am born dominated by the wood energy when it retreats in an unbalanced way as it is directed sideways in the deep mountain glens. The wood energy governs the first growth of things, and so these antlers grow in an unbalanced way, like a tree's branches, from my head. At the same time, I have a damp nature. The energy that governs the first appearance of things and their subsequent growth also governs the first movements of consciousness. That's why the flesh at the base of my horns resembles the writing of ideographs.

"Certain people of the World of Law mistake these patterns for actual writing and conclude that they are messages from the gods. Based on the explanations of these patterns, the writings of Shinto have been assembled, known as *The Great Compilation*.[38] But that compilation is woven together around the theory of the five elements, and it speaks nothing of the True and Subtle Way of the Gods, based as it is on the four elements, which advance and retreat as mutual natures. These Shinto priests start with their own foolish speculations and deluded beliefs and then go on to delude the world at large. They are of my ilk. I am the Shinto priest of the World of Beasts, and the Shinto priests are the Deer of the World of Law."

The Boar, who was lying down in the gathering, lifted his head to say: "I am born of the unbalanced motion of the sideways energy in its retreating phase in the mountain glens, and I eat snakes, frogs, worms, and other creatures that live in such damp places. When I charge, I run at full strength, but when I must move either to the side or backward, I lose my vigor, and I lack the ability to think far into the future.

"There are those in the World of Law who have plenty of strength when they face an enemy, but lack the ability to think broadly, to see far into the future, and to make plans or strategies. Without realizing that it will be their own undoing, these blind generals foolishly destroy rice fields and farm plots. They are of my ilk. I am the blind general of the World of Beasts, and the fierce generals of the World of Law are Wild Boars."

The Rhinoceros with his single horn appeared from one side of the assembly and said: "I was born from sideways energy of mountain glens. I have a single horn and I eat nuts, berries, fruits, and small animals. In turn, I am the prey of larger beasts. The Goat Antelope is my companion, yet I steal and eat the food that he has stored away.

"There are people in the World of Law who imitate me. They neglect their own work and spend all their energies scheming to steal the property of others. These are of my ilk."

Now the Ram was at the rear of the assembly, his horns resting on the ground. After hearing the opinions of so many beasts, he stepped forward to voice his own. "I am born of the gentle sideways energy of mountain valleys, so my flesh is tender and delicious and I am fat. The sideways energy is very strong in me, and so my heart is dominated by it. I deceive those below me and greedily devour their food. Not only do I violate the females of other beasts, but I teach other beasts to do likewise. The sages who established the World of Law are just like me, with minds dominated by the sideways energy. They do not cultivate but thieve Heaven's Way and the realm. They plant the roots of thievery and strife. They put themselves over all others, and they deceive those below them, greedily devouring their food. Since they are of the same energy as I, they are extraordinarily fond

51

of my flesh. They keep sheep and eat our meat morning and night. They are so passionately fond of it that they combined the characters for "sheep" 羊 and "big" 大 to form the character for "beauty" 美 . All things that they regard beautiful—delicacies of the table, clothing, women, furnishings, flowers, and, decorations—all are described by a character meaning "big sheep." This proves that the sages are none other than Rams like me. I am the Sage of the World of Beasts, and the sages of the World of Law are Rams."

The Musk Deer was on the west side of the gathering, and its odor was so terribly strong that the heads of many of the beasts began to ache. Complaints could be heard throughout the assembly. "You must move out of the breeze." "Yes, humans may like your odor, but for us beasts it is most unpleasant."

The Musk Deer spoke up. "I am full to overflowing of a great deal of the warm, damp energy of the sideways energy. My heart and my stomach are both roasted by that energy, and I can't myself bear the smell I give off. The hotter it is the worse I smell, and sometimes it grows so bad that my own stomach bursts. For this reason, I cannot keep company with other beasts, and I live the life of one abandoned in the fields.

"There are in the World of Law those who are frightfully full of a festering, damp, evil energy, so that the flesh of their faces rots. Their condition is called leprosy, and they are denied the company of other humans; they are abandoned and left to live on their own, as beggars and outcasts. These ones are of my ilk."

The Goat Antelope spoke. "I am born of a strong sideways energy of the mountain glens. The water energy in me is weak, and so I can't see very well. But my four legs are strong and I know many kinds of trees. In autumn and winter I eat the bark of those trees and in spring and summer I eat a variety of smaller creatures. I can prance about on rocks and boulders, and even perch on their tips. I know what's good and bad about each tree in each season, and I use that knowledge to eat their bark.

"In the World of Law there are those, too, who know well the good and bad points of all sorts of trees, and with that knowledge are able to make good use of those trees. These are the carpenters and woodcarvers, and they are of my ilk."

The Pig was in a corner of assembly. The Dog addressed him: "You are well-liked by all the beasts, and clever at flattery. Please let us hear what you have to say." The Pig began. "I was born of a combination of the surplus energies of Dog and Deer, and I am very weak. Therefore, I make my living by deceiving and flattering this one, then deceiving and flattering that one. In the World of Law the merchants share my lot. In their profession, flattery and deception prevail even among parents and children, as the merchants pursue their singleminded course of profit, flattering those above and deceiving those below, all for their own benefit. They do this in imitation of me. I am the merchant of the World of Beasts, and merchants are the Pigs of the World of Law."

The Monkey screamed down from his elevated perch: "I am born from the energy of the fruits of forest trees. The fruits of trees grow from the surplus energy of grain. That is why my form resembles that

of humans (who are born from the energy of grain). But I am also full of the sideways energy of mountain glens, and so I resemble a beast as well. While my body is that of a beast, my face and my hands and feet are those of a human. I am neither man nor beast. I sit on the border between them, always busily munching fruits.

"There are those in the World of Law whose hearts are dominated by the sideways energy, though they have human form. They do not cultivate, but thieve Heaven's Way and greedily devour them. Though they appear to be humans, dominated by the upward energy, their actions and hearts are those of beasts, dominated by the sideways energy. These people who greedily consume without cultivating, starting with the sages, Shakyamuni, Laozi, and Prince Shotoku, are all of my ilk. I am the Great Patriarch of the laws of the six teachings in the World of Beasts, and the patriarchs of the six teachings in the World of Law are Monkeys."[39]

The Baboon is born from the spirit of ancient trees in deep, shrouded mountain valleys, and is extremely rare, so none had come to join the assembly of the beasts.

Then came a great leaping company of Leopards, as fast as if flying. The beasts were all frightened, and as they were looking to see what it was that was fast upon them, one Leopard took an upper seat in the assembly and growled in a loud voice. "I am the Leopard, the footsoldier

54

of the World of Beasts. I belong to the tribe of the Tiger and I am born of the sideways metal energy of mountain glens. The Horse is the footsoldier of domestic animals, but I am the footsoldier of the wild beasts. O beasts! Do not fail to obey the orders of your ruler. If anyone should resist, I will catch him and devour him!

"The footsoldiers of the World of Law greedily devour all the people below them, and this is because they are of my ilk."

The Wolf arrived next, baring his fangs, and he took a slightly raised seat at the front of the assembly. After letting out a long howl, he said: "I am born dominated by the sideways stone and wood energies of the mountain glens. I am the Wolf, the retainer of the feudal lord of the World of Beasts, Lord Tiger. Leopards, have you made the imperial order known to all the beasts? If anyone should dare to resist, I will tear him to bits."

The beasts all cowered in fear, and the Wolf continued. "In the World of Law, too, there are those warriors who live off the labors of the footsoldiers. They are of my ilk. I am the retainer of the World of Beasts, and the retainers of the World of Law are Wolves."

Then the Bear lumbered in and stopped at the front, before the Wolf. In a great loud voice he declared: "I am born dominated by the sideways energy of water of the mountain glens. I am the Bear, the senior retainer of the World of Beasts. I will snatch and devour each and every  beast who defies the orders of their superiors. There are senior retainers among the people of the World of Law as well, and they live off the efforts of the ordinary retainers below them. I am the senior retainer of the World of Beasts, and all senior retainers of the World of Law are Bears."

The beasts saw clearly the sharp strong claws of the Bear and bowed in terror. Just then the Tiger accompanied by a great company of Tigers came thundering in like a great storm. The Tiger found a place for himself atop a boulder in the bamboo grove at the front of the assembly, and facing the gathered beasts, he raised his head and roared. "I am born dominated by the sideways metal energy of the mountain glens. I am the Tiger, the feudal lord of the World of Beasts. Senior retainers and retainers, have you made clear the orders of our ruler?"

The Wolf and the Bear bowed low and replied, "Yes we have, my liege." The Tiger added. "If you are lax in your duties, I will tear you to shreds.

"Among the people of the World of Law there are feudal lords, too. They live off the efforts of their senior retainers and retainers. Thus I am the lord of the World of Beasts, and the feudal lord of the World of Law are Tigers."

All the beasts were filled with terror by the Tiger's ferocious appear-

ance, when the Lion arrived in a great flurry, accompanied by a pride of attendant Lions. They sped faster than flight and the leading Lion leapt up onto the precipice of a boulder at the front of the assembly and let out a mighty roar. The Tiger, the Bear, the Wolf, and all the other beasts pressed themselves to the earth, so fearful that their hearts might stop.

The Lion spoke. "I am born dominated by the metal and fire energies of the mountain glens and am the generalissimo of the World of Beasts. Should any one of you resist my will, I'll have done with you in an instant."

Just then in the distance could be seen the *Doku,* with a great, fierce, and noisome following of attendant *Doku,* making his way to the gathering. As all the beasts from the Lion on down were watching, expecting the arrival of the ruler of all beasts, the Elephant arrived. The Elephant first stopped at an enormous boulder on the south side of the assembly and said in a gentle voice: "I am born dominated by the damp sideways energy of mountain glens. I am huge and fat, my nose is long, and my ears droop down like a crown. I am the aristocrat of the World of Beasts. All of you, from the Lion on down, do not neglect your respective duties. If anyone dares to do so, I will report that beast to the emperor, who will devour him.

"Among the people of the World of Law, there are also aristocrats and nobles. They live off the labors of the generalissimo and the feudal lords. The aristocrat of the World of Beasts is none other than me, and the aristocrats of the World of Law are Elephants."

The *Doku* had by now arrived and with his great party of smaller, attendant *Doku* took a place on the north of the great boulder at the front of the assembly. Facing the south, he let loose with a single great howl that rose to the Heavens, shook the mountains and rivers, and was so huge and penetrating that the Lion and all the other beasts were temporarily struck deaf. They were paralyzed by the sound, and so terrified that they weren't certain whether they were alive or dead.

After a moment the *Doku* began to speak. "I am born dominated by the sideways energy and the advancing phase of the fire energy of

the mountain glens. My fundamental nature is indestructible metal (which shares mutual natures with the fire energy). I am the emperor of the beasts. There are no beasts above me, which is why I am called the One and Only *(doku)*. All the beasts of the earth are my subjects. I lead ten thousand chariots, and Elephants are my food.

"Among the people of the World of Law, there is also an emperor. He lives off the labors of the aristocrats below him and shares my lot. Thus I am the emperor of the World of Beasts, and the emperor of the World of Law is a *Doku.*"

The *Doku* continued. "Among all those below me there is a definite order and hierarchy. The rule that larger eats smaller derives from the circulation of Heaven's Truth in a sideways direction. It is not a failing of the World of Beasts. Humans, however, though born in a world of Right Cultivation in which Heaven's Truth circulates in an upward direction, refuse to cultivate. Instead they thieve Heaven's Way and willfully transform the world into the World of Law. There, the emperor devours the fruits of the aristocrats' labors, the generalissimo devours the fruits of the feudal lords' labors, the feudal lords devour the fruits of their retainers' labors, the retainers devour the fruits of the footsoldiers' labors, the footsoldiers devour the fruits of the populace's labors, and, among the people, the master devours the fruits of his servants' labors. This hierarchy in which larger eats smaller was created in imitation of the World of Beasts. That human beings, who are born in a world of upward energy, should behave like beasts, who are dominated by the sideways energy, is because their hearts have come under the lopsided, deluded sway of the sideways energy. This was all begun by the sages and Shakyamuni." (The details of this are described at length in the earlier record of the assembly of the birds.)

"Though beasts eat each other, beasts do not capture other beasts alive, pen them up, and keep them. The sages and wise men of the World of Law, though, do just this, and then kill these beasts, declaring that it is for their own nourishment, or as a sacrifice to Heaven. Can there be any god in Heaven who would rejoice at having the very beasts that he gave life to killed and offered up to him? Is there any Sage or wise man who would rejoice to have, for example, his own child killed and then offered to him as a sacrifice, or as tribute?

"Ahh, these sages, greatly deluded because of the sideways energy they have fallen under the sway of, don't even grasp as simple a principle as this, such are the twisted hearts they are born with. As a result of their delusion, they have turned the human world, which is essentially one of the upward energy and Right Cultivation in accord with Heaven's Truth, into the World of Law, which is exactly like the World of Beasts, dominated by sideways energy.

"Beasts that are caught and kept in cages for a long time cannot undergo the natural changes that they should at the proper times, and they die. Even if they are set free and allowed to return to the wild they cannot return to their original wild state, and in the end they grow thin and weak and they die. This is because they have been too long in contact with the upward energy of human beings, and their natural sideways energy as beasts has been impaired. A Leopard, for example, who is caught and caged for a long time and then set free in the wilds will grow thin and weak and will die; just so, a footsoldier of the World of Law who loses his post and no longer collects his pay will fall to begging and the deepest poverty. Any beast that is caught and kept too long in a cage will be unable to survive when returned to the wild, and will eventually grow thin and weak and will die; just so, the senior retainer or feudal lord of the World of Law who is defeated in battle, or the generalissimo, the aristocrat, or the emperor who is overthrown in an uprising and must hide among the people, all of these will suffer the same fate. Thus it is that the World of Beasts and the World of Law are identical.

"Beasts have minds dominated by the sideways energy, and so a beast may, in his natural ignorance, come up with the deluded thought that with his four legs he is no different from a human being, who also has four limbs. But when he stands up, all he can see are the Heavens directly above. Nothing of what lies before or behind him is visible. He will then regret his foolishness and drop back down to his natural sideways position. The people of the World of Law—the sages, Shakyamuni, the many great teachers, the monks, and all men of learning—come up with the deluded thought that they are better than all other humans, and with minds only for elevated wisdom they seek the meanings of difficult and distant writings, and thus fail to grasp the Subtle Way of mutual natures that lies within themselves. In other words, they can't see what's in front of them, no different from the deluded beasts who rise up on two legs. This is because both groups have minds dominated by the sideways energy."

The Dog of the World of Beasts then said, "When, due to the

activities of the world's energies, the desire to mate arises within us Dogs, dogs and bitches pair off and howl and bark at each other. This is the way we enjoy our love play. The men and women of the world intent on lovemaking pair off, too, and they sing and dance, pluck the koto and strum the samisen. Their way of enjoying their love play is an imitation of ours." The Wolf added, "When the desire to mate arises within us Wolves, we howl with the four tones of the Chinese language: even, rising, falling, and rising and falling. The people of the World of Law, in imitation of our cries during the mating period, created the four musical modes that they use to compose music for poetry-chanting and the Noh drama. The ones who do this are of our ilk."

The Tiger spoke up. "When our mating period arrives, we roar with great gusts of air, and this roaring sounds like nothing more than the echoes of a metal flute. In imitation of our mating call, the sages of the World of Law created the music of court ceremonial, and they are of our ilk."

The Cat spoke next. "When, in accord with the movements of Heaven-and-Earth, our mating period arrives, we cry out and wail in voices that rise and fall in pitch and volume to attract our mates. The people of the World of Law, in our imitation, sing and chant that music of the puppet theater. Their melodies and declamations are the same as our rising and falling mating cries."

The Horse of the spring pasture added. "We horses of both sexes, stallions and mares, when our mating season comes, grow so mad with lust that we forget all else, even the threat of death. There are people in the World of Law who are like us; they fall so deeply into lust for women that they undo themselves, they lose all sense of shame and forget even death. They are the ilk of us horses of the spring pastures."

The Fox joined in. "When I eat too many mulberries, I grow intoxicated. I retch, my mind grows clouded, and I fall into a wild and crazed state. Though my companions bark and yap at me, I can't remember anything that's happened. There are those like me in the World of Law. They lose themselves in women and drink until they grow ill, and though they are ruining their lives, they aren't in the least aware of it. These ones are of my ilk."

He continued. "When the Wolf has caught me and is about to devour me, I set fire to his eyelashes with the foxfire that burns in my tail. In the human World of Law there are people who, when they are driven to desperation by the heavy taxes and tribute squeezed from them by their rulers, set fire to people's homes and loot them while they're burning. These are of my ilk."

The Bear wanted to add his part. "I hide in holes in the trunks of trees, and when another Bear passes by, I set upon him, kill him, and eat him. Among the people of the World of Law, there are those who lie in wait along the highways and set upon and kill travelers passing by, making their living by stealing the possessions of their victims. These are of my ilk.

"In fact, all the activities of the people of the World of Law are exactly like those of us of the World of Beasts. There is not the slightest difference between them. This is because the human heart twisted and unbalanced by the sideways energy acts in the same way as the sideways energy under which we beasts are naturally born."

And so the beasts came to the following conclusion:

"Though the World of Law and the World of Beasts are in many respects the same, there are some differences. There is no end to the delusion of men's hearts that causes such thievery and strife in the World of Law. As a result, an emperor, a generalissimo, a feudal lord, or a senior retainer who is defeated in battle will be reduced to a beggar or an outcast. On the other hand, an ordinary citizen or soldier can, by triumphing in battle, become an emperor, a generalissimo, or a great feudal lord. There are, too, among ordinary people, those who lose their fortunes and are reduced to beggary; and those, too, who make a fortune and grow rich. Among Buddhist monks it is the same: a high-ranking monk can be driven from his monastery and become a wandering beggar monk.

"In years of bad harvest, more than half of the people may die of starvation. Corpses cover the land. There are those who are so poor that they are forced to sell their homes and abandon the land. There are those who suffer terribly under the burden of loans. There are those with piles of money who sigh with pleasure that this world is a veritable paradise. There are those, too, who lack the smallest pittance, and moan and lament that this world is hell.

"These innumerable sufferings are to be found in the World of Law, but not in the World of Beasts. The sages and Shakyamuni have said that those who know not the law are mere beasts. But in our lawless World of Beasts, the emperor of the beasts can never be reduced to a beggar beast. We beasts undergo various changes and transformations according to the laws of life and death, and the fates of the people of the World of Law also undergo many changes, all due to the ravages of thievery and strife. Yet in the World of Beasts there is no need to worry about bad harvests or famine, or of being able to scrape together the annual tax and tribute, or of repaying loans. No beast is forced to sell his home or abandon his territory because of poverty. There is no need to worry about arson and looting. We beasts are free from the evils of flattery and scorn, and we have no place in either paradise or hell. The World of Beasts is a peaceful one, far superior to the human World of Law."

Since there is no gold or silver in the World of Beasts, thievery and strife, the delusions of lust, are nowhere to be found.

Third Session

THE CRAWLING CREATURES

GATHER TO DISCUSS THE WORLD OF LAW

The creatures of damp places, the creatures born of the air, metamorphosing creatures, shelled creatures, creatures of human homes, creatures of human settlements, creatures of the fields, creatures of the rivers and streams, creatures of the mountains, and creatures of the seas—all existing creatures gathered, each to take its turn in discussing the human World of Law.

The Sea Turtle began by proclaiming: "The Dragon exists in name only; it is no more than another name for the yang energy. From time to time, a small scaled creature about four or five inches in length that resembles depictions of dragons is born in deep caves in the moun-

tains. After a specified period of the circulation of energy, it metamorphoses into a creature of damp places. The Dragon is just a depiction of this creature writ large, and in fact the Dragon is not to be found in our World of Creatures.

"I have a shell, and with my mysterious powers I am the leader of the World of Creatures. I dwell in the great seas and live for ages. I am the emperor of the World of Creatures. The Terrapin is the aristocrat of the World of Creatures, the Python is our generalissimo. The Centipedes are our feudal lords, the Serpents our retainers. The

Wasps are the footsoldiers of the World of Creatures, and the Ants are the spies. I am the greatest, and I devour Turtles smaller than me. The Terrapin eats the small Vipers below him. The Python eats the Centipedes below him. The Centipedes consume the Serpents below them. The Serpents eat the Frogs below them, and the Wasps eat the smaller insects below them, and thus on down the line. This is the order in which large creatures eat small creatures, and small creatures eat still smaller creatures, on down through the hierarchy in just this fashion. This is the Truth of Heaven as it is provided to the World of Creatures.

"Though we are grouped together as creatures, we are actually of several different origins. The creatures of damp places are born from outgrowths of the surplus energy of beasts; winged creatures are born from outgrowths of the surplus energy of birds. That is why large devours small in our World of Creatures, just as in the worlds of birds and beasts. And since this is an order natural to us, the small creatures do not greatly fear the larger ones. The World of Creatures is an outgrowth of the sideways circulation of energy, as it manifests itself in the worlds of birds and beasts.

"Although the World of Human Beings was originally one governed by the upward circulation of energy, certain human beings born with a nature of unbalanced purity fell under the governance of the sideways circulation of energy and created self-serving laws, establishing the World of Law. As a result, the World of Human Beings has become the same as our World of Creatures. Unbalanced energy, unbalanced minds, and unbalanced behavior are all the products of the sideways energy. The hierarchy of the human World of

Law, in which large devours small, is exactly like the hierarchy in our World of Creatures, in which large devours small. And thus it is that the actions of human beings in the World of Law are no different from those of us creatures."

The Serpent's seat was in the lower part of the middle section of the assembly, and he slithered forth on his belly from it. "I am born with a great deal of dampness and thus I can make no sound. All I can do is hiss through my nose. I am poisonous. As the retainer of the World of Creatures, it is my role to attack and kill with my poison fangs those who would disobey the commands of their rulers. In the human World of Law there are also retainers, who extort from the people the fruits of their Right Cultivation and slash to pieces with their great swords whoever should resist. These are of my ilk, and so it is that I am the retainer of the World of Creatures and the retainers of the World of Law are poisonous serpents."

The Centipede was seated in the middle section of the assembly. He rolled forward on his hundred legs and spoke: "I am born in rock caves and have a great amount of the fire energy in me; the aspect of movement associated with that energy is so fulsome in me that it has produced my hundred legs. I am the feudal lord of the World of Creatures, and all you creatures know: I will kill and eat each and every creature who dares to disobey the law of the realm. Among the human beings of the World of Law there are also feudal lords, who catch and kill whoever dares

to oppose the government of the realm. So it is that I am the feudal lord of the World of Creatures, and the feudal lords of the World of Law are centipedes."

The lordly Python was in the upper portion of the middle section of the assembly. His great voice resounded: "I was born of a surplus of the wood energy of the dampness of the mountains, and I am the generalissimo of the World of Creatures. Should any of you Centipedes fail to pay me regular homage by attending on me in my den, I will change your place of residence, devour and destroy you. You lesser creatures, should you behave willfully, I will seize and eat you on the spot. Among the human beings of the World of Law there is the generalissimo. He consumes the labors of the feudal lords below him, and he is of my ilk. So it is that I am the generalissimo of the World of Creatures, and the generalissimo of the World of Law is a great Python."

The Terrapin was in an upper seat. In a quiet and refined voice he ventured: "I am born of the unbalanced sideways circulation of the receding phase of the metal energy in the ocean. My shell is pure and translucent, and I am the aristocrat of the World of Creatures. O Python! Be always certain not to violate the commands of our emperor the Sea Turtle! Should you be lax in your duties, you will be killed with the emperor's water torture. Among the human beings of the World of Law there are aristocrats as well, who receive the orders of the emperor and convey them to the generalissimo. So it is that I am the aristocrat of the World of Creatures, and the aristocrat of the World of Law is a Terrapin."

The Sea Turtle's clear voice rang out from the highest seat of the assembly: "I am born of the pure, bright energy in the sea. I am the emperor of the World of Creatures. You, O Terrapin, take care to transmit my imperial commands to the ministers below, and dare you not be lax in your duties. Should you be lax, I will devour you. Since I am the emperor of the World of Creatures, there is no creature more dominated by the sideways energy, of more unbalanced mind or intellect than me. In the World of Law there is an emperor as well. He, too, was born with a nature of unbalanced purity and was under the unbalanced domination of sideways energy. Thus [like Fuxi] his heart and his mind were unbalanced, and he created the practice of divination. All emperors and sages are born dominated by the same energy as myself and have unbalanced hearts. The system of divination is an unbalanced error; Shennong's *Classic of Herbal Natural History*, Huang Di's calendar, Yao's supplemented and revised calendar, the writings of Yao and Shun, Yu's mysterious floodwater inscription[40]–all these are the products of my sideways energy. Likewise, the classics of Tang and Wen were created by means of the unbalanced minds of the sage-emperors. All these writings are unbalanced and erroneous, and their authors are of my ilk.

"Thus we can see that I am the emperor of the World of Creatures, dominated as I am by unbalanced energy. The emperors of the World of Law, in generation after generation, are Sea Turtles, dominated by unbalanced energy. From this we may know that each and every teaching and writing of these sage-emperors is an unbalanced error. Unbalanced error is the root of thievery and revolt, and they are the root of all evils and delusions. All derive from the unbalanced nature of the sideways energy. All you creatures large and small, contemplate this truth and do not imitate the World of Law."

The Wasp was pressed to the earth at the back of the assembly. It turned to the other creatures and spoke: "I am born of the mutual natures of fire and metal in summer and autumn. I have a barb in my tail, and I am the footsoldier of the World of Creatures. If any of you smaller creatures should dare to disobey your rulers' commands I will sting and kill you. Among the human beings of the World of Law there are also footsoldiers, who cut down and kill any who dare to disobey the law. So it is that I am the footsoldier of the World of Creatures, and the footsoldiers of the World of Law are wasps."

The Ant was in a hole at one side of the assembly. He crept out and spoke up: "I am born of the metal energy in summer, as it circulates in an unbalanced sideways fashion. My mandibles are sharp and my waist trim. I am the spy of the World of Creatures. I keep watch on all the creatures of our world, large and small, and this is what I see: Each follows the nature given it at birth. Each eats that which is provided it by heaven, the things of its place of birth. Each makes its skin, hair, or wings its robes, each builds a nest for its home, as shelter from wind and rain. Creatures born on the leaves of plants eat those leaves; creatures born in damp earth eat earth; creatures born inside tree trunks eat wood. Each eats the thing of its place of birth, each makes its own efforts to acquire that food. This is the Right Cultivation of the World of Creatures. The worlds of birds, beasts, and fishes are in this all alike. None rejects the lot provided it by Heaven's Truth. Only the human beings of the World of Law refuse to cultivate, reject the lot provided them by Heaven's Truth, establish self-serving laws, and thieve and devour the cultivation of Heaven's Way. Though born under the governance of the upward energy, their behavior is worse than that of those born under the governance of the sideways energy. They indulge in thievery, revolt, and delusion. It is my role to spy, and I have spied this out. So it is that I am the spy of the World of Creatures. Yet the spies of the World of Law cannot spy what even an ant can see."

The Tree Frog sat at one side of the assembly. Feeling that rain was on its way he hopped out with his reedy croak: "I am born of the essence of dampness. My arms and legs resemble those of a human being. The larger ones of my kind are called toads. When rain prepares to fall,  the dampness in me responds sympathetically and with my reedy trill I give vent to my thoughts and feelings. My trilling in turn leads other creatures to express their feelings as well, and so I give pleasure to the World of Creatures. Among the human beings of the World of Law there was one [Confucius] who composed the *Book of Songs,* in which he praised fathers, brothers, and sisters-in-law and gave great importance to graceful expression.[41] He set his odes to melodies and led all in the realm in singing them, encouraging them to indulge their emotions and to be remiss in their Right Cultivation. He did not know that in doing so he invited chaos nor that his odes were the expressions of the delusion bred of the sideways energy.

"My trilling is my birthright. I give vent to my feelings in response to the circulations of energy in Heaven and Earth. Human beings of the True World are born of the upward energy, and they are governed by the upward energy. They are not provided by nature with the need to indulge their emotions or to glorify their own delusions. The human beings of the World of Law have suppressed their upward energy and aroused the sideways energy to govern them, and this is why they are attached to the glorification of their unbalanced minds and deluded hearts; unbalanced by the sideways energy, they indulge their emotions and give vent to their feelings. These expressions of their indulgent emotions they shape into odes. And so it is that composing odes is nothing other than glorifying the delusion caused by overindulged emotions, which leads to falling into one of the four realms dominated by the sideways energy.

"The Duke of Zhou was the first to compose such odes. Later, the learned men of the Qin and Han dynasties imitated him in creating the rules of poetry composition. Later still, the learned men of the Tang, Song, and Ming dynasties again imitated their forebears as well as imitating the *Classic of Rhymes* by the Indian monk Shen Gong, and they devoted themselves with great energy to rhymed verse. This came to be regarded as an elevated field of study and was transmitted to Korea and Japan. All the scholars who follow in these footsteps indulge their emotions and glorify their own delusions, falling into the four realms. The scholars who do not know this and devote themselves to composing poetry are all of my ilk. So it is that I am the Duke of Zhou, and the poets of every land through the ages, of the World of Creatures. The Duke of Zhou and the poets through the ages of the World of Law are all Tree Frogs."

The Army Ant was on the eastern side of the assembly. He came forward to speak his part. "I am born in holes in soft earth from the sideways energy of metal during the hottest part of summer. There is much fire energy, which shares mutual natures with the metal energy, in me, and by nature I am a stickler for proper observance of rites [, which corresponds to the element fire in the five-element theory]. On sunny days I make my rounds searching for food; when the wind blows or the snow falls, I seek shelter from the weather in the hole in the earth that I make my home. There I mate with my partner and we produce offspring who will succeed to our way of life.

"When on my rounds for food I chance to meet one of my kind I bend my narrow waist in a bow and go on my way, making room for my fellow. When I find a morsel I stay my course until I have eaten it, and then I move on in search again. Thus my life and the summer pass. Oh yes—and sometimes while I'm in my hole, I compose writings influenced by my sideways intellect.

"Among the human beings of the World of Law there was one [Confucius] who from birth was fond of bending at the waist. He stole the fruits of the Right Cultivation of others and, without cultivating himself, greedily devoured them. All his life he wandered from kingdom to kingdom, seeking a stipend. When a would-be patron stopped him and offered him a stipend, he stayed his course; when there was no stipend, he moved on to another kingdom. In the end he was never to receive a lasting stipend and he retreated into his own home, where he composed many works that were expressions of his sideways mind, and he consigned them to posterity. All of his words are unbalanced and deluded, but they resulted in the widespread practice in later ages of humanity and righteousness, rewards and punishment, which in turn were the source of unending thievery and revolt. So it is that I am the Confucius of the World of Creatures, and the Confucius of the World of Law was an army ant."

The Leech was at the side of the upper portion of the assembly, for which the Salamander reprimanded him. After a pause the Leech replied: "I am born of the soft dampness of the mud, so my body itself is extremely soft. When I contract, I am as small and round as a bean. When I  stretch out, I extend myself to both front and back. But as I am slimy and slippery, I don't make much progress either forward or backward. I think of myself as the Mean, and I know that it is Heaven's Rule that has allowed me to achieve this Mean. It is said that in the Way of Truth there can be no Mean, but I regard the Way of the Mean as the most elevated path of all. In the passages that make up many writings, the word "Mean" appears countless times, yet the Mean is not an expression used to describe the True Way. I, however, have taken this mere convention of expression and made it the very source of the Way because I am dominated by the sideways energy.

"Among the human beings of the World of Law, one [of Confucius's descendants, Zisi,] composed a work entitled *The Doctrine of the Mean*.[42] He claimed that that which is ordained by Heaven's command is called the essential nature of all phenomena. He knew nothing of the fact that the natures of all phenomena are mutual. He defined the Mean as the state in which neither joy nor anger nor sadness nor pleasure had yet arisen. He was ignorant of the fact that the natures of the four emotions joy, anger, sadness, and pleasure are mutual manifestations of energy. There is no possibility of the existence of a Mean in the True Way.

"That the True Way unfolds as mutual natures is clearly demonstrated by the eight gates of our faces.[43] The lack of any Mean in mutual natures is given ample proof by this empirical observation. Since Zisi was ignorant of this, he was of my ilk. I am the Zisi of the World of Creatures, and Zisi was the Leech of the World of Law."

The Toad was in northern seat, from which he launched out. "I am born from the strong damp energy in the mountains. My body is large and my big eyes bulge out. My arms have a shoulder joint, an elbow, and a wrist, and my hand five fingers. I have a pelvis, knees, and ankles,  five toes, and a stomach and a back, just like a human being. If I walk upright, I am no different from a person. And so it is that I call on Heaven with this plea: Let me become a human being! In this teeming assembly of creatures, let me stand and walk upright!"

He stood, but all he could see was the Heavens above. He lost the faculty for distinguishing among things. Unable to see what lay in front of him, he was greatly inconvenienced and terribly handicapped. The Toad regretted his arrogance profoundly, and cried out, "Heaven, pardon me! Pray return me to my original sideways way of walking!" After a moment, with a great sigh of relief, he was restored to his natural position. The assembly of creatures laughed uproariously. In great embarrassment, the Toad spoke. "I am not the only one to be so foolish. Among the human beings of the World of Law, the eleven sages, the many wise men, Shakyamuni and the Buddhist patriarchs, the many learned monks, Laozi, Zhuangzi, Prince Shotoku, and the scholars of literature in age after age—all of them tried and schemed to attain a high level of intellect. But since all of them were dominated by the sideways energy, they regarded their sideways minds and intellects as elevated and far reaching. They mistook their deluded sideways-ranging feelings as feelings of great depth and of great height, reaching beyond Heaven. Looking only to the heights, they failed to see the eight organs of their own faces, which reveal the Subtle Way of Complementarity. This is being unable to see what is in front of one's face. It is an extreme handicap, a delusion, and a glorification of delusion. So it is that they are of my ilk. I am the great master of the sages, Shakyamuni, Laozi, Zhuangzi, and all learned ones of the World of Creatures. The sages, Shakyamuni, Laozi and Zhuangzi, and all the learned men of the World of Law are Toads."

The Toad repented his error of imitating human beings, entreated Heaven, was forgiven, and returned to his original state as a Toad. The sages, Shakyamuni, and all the learned ones are so unbalanced in their delusion that they aren't aware that they are imitating Toads. They do not regret their folly and so will fall into birth as Toads for infinity, unable to return ever to their original human form. Thus it is that the learned men of the world are less than Toads. How tragic, indeed.

The Little Ant inched forward to speak from the back of the assembly. "I am born of an outgrowth of the surplus energy of the Army Ant. I am like the Army Ant, and when I meet one of my kind I bow and step aside to let him pass. I stop for a moment when I find food; if there is no food, I move on. This is my life; in general, I follow the path of the Army Ant.

"Among the human beings of the World of Law, there was one

[Mencius] who followed the path of former learned ones. He roamed from kingdom to kingdom, selling 'humanity and righteousness' here and 'the cultivation of the all-encompassing energy (*ki*)' there. He did not cultivate for himself but greedily devoured the fruits of other's Right Cultivation according to Heaven's Way. When someone offered to support him, he stopped for a moment. If no one provided him with a stipend, he went on to another kingdom. That was his life, and he was of my ilk. I am the Mencius of the World of Creatures, and the Mencius of the World of Law was a Little Ant."

The Salamander was resting in a little hollow of the assembly when the creatures urged him to come forward. "I am born," he began, "of the hard dampness in the water and I am made up of a combination of the fire and water energies, so my belly is red and my back is black. I live in water and eat tiny insects. Though water is soft, it is hard to violate it, and peaceful-

ness is my virtue. So it is that with my unbalanced sideways mind I have concluded that water is the origin of Heaven-and-Earth, of human beings, and of all things, including myself. There is nothing more hallowed than water, I am convinced, but since my intelligence is unbalanced by the sideways energy I remain ignorant of the mutual nature of water. There was one [Laozi] in the World of Law, too, who regarded water as the source of Heaven-and-Earth, human beings, and all things and claimed that there is nothing more hallowed than water—"the mystery of mysteries, the Great Way of the Void," he called it. He, who remained ignorant of the nature of water, who loved water like a goose, he was of my ilk. So it is that I am the Laozi of the World of Creatures, and Laozi was a Salamander."

The Water Boatman was at one side of the assembly. After listening to the various creatures speak he stepped forward. "I am born of the energy of the foam on the water's surface. I sail over the water faster than flight. The water is soft and doesn't resist, and it permits me to float, so that I romp as if through the Heavens. Truly water's non-active virtue of the Way is supreme. I greatly respect the Salamander's words.

"Among the human beings of the World of Law, one [Zhuangzi] respected Laozi's delusions concerning water and grew deluded himself. He took water as representing the non-active virtue of the Way and spun all sorts of crazy tales. But all of these tales showed an ignorance of water, and his intelligence was no different from mine. So it is that I am the Zhuangzi of the World of Creatures, and Zhuangzi was a Water Boatman."

The Grasshopper was at the south side of the assembly. It came forth just as the assembly fell silent in a brief intermission. "I am born from the damp air that accumulates in thick patches of grass. I drink

mist and eat the soft, ripe seeds of grasses. This is my Right Cultivation. On sunny days I climb up onto the leaves of plants, look about, ponder the view, and think elegant thoughts. I give sentimental vent to my feelings and express my thoughts by painting pictures on leaves. As my emotions reach their peak my self-control dissolves and, in harmony with the workings of Heaven, I begin to cry. This is my lot, a result of my birth under the domination of the sideways energy.

"Among the human beings of the World of Law, there are those whose minds are unbalanced by the sideways energy, though that is not their birthright. Deluded thus, they contemplate the scenery, lose their thoughts and their wills to the things around them, and indulge their emotions. They take great pains in selecting the right words to express their feelings and lose themselves in searching for the proper rhymes and rhythms, ignorant of the Subtle Inherence of mutual natures in the unfolding of sounds. They only pay attention to the sound of the words as they utter them to themselves, composing their odes and selecting their words. These poets who suppress their upward energy and allow themselves to be governed by the sideways energy, indulge their emotions, and grow deluded and confused are of my ilk. So it is that I am the poet of the World of Creatures, and the poets of the World of Law are Grasshoppers."

The Earthworm came wriggling out from a corner of the assembly. "I am born of the energy of soft dampness in the earth, and soft earth is my food. I am always as if bound by the soft earth, and my movements are not free. When the circulation of the energy of the season and  culation of the energy within me are in harmony, I make tiny noises. There are Buddhist monks in the World of Law who do not cultivate but greedily devour the fruits of Heaven's Way. They establish their own sect and with rules of discipline and morality they bind themselves so that their movements are not free. These are of my ilk.

I am the Ritsu- sect monk of the World of Creatures, and the Ritsu monks of the World of Law are Earthworms."[44]

The Lizard was at the north side of the assembly. He came scampering out to say: "I am born of the thin, damp energy among the grass, and I am wrapped with the metal energy. That is why my body shines, and I have golden stripes as well. There are Buddhist monks in the World of Law who wear shiny gold and gold-striped vestments—the monks of the Jojitsu sect. They are of my ilk. So it is that I am the Jojitsu monk of the World of Creatures, and the Jojitsu monks of the World of Law are Lizards."[45]

The Spider was hiding in a corner of the room. All the creatures turned to it and inquired in a chorus: "Why, why, in this great assembly of all the creatures, do you hide? Come out and speak up." So the Spider came out and spoke up: "I am born of the stagnant energy that collects in corners and crevices, and I can unfurl long coils of that stagnant energy from of my body. My stomach is full of thread. I spin my web with it and with my web I trap the flying insects that happen to pass. After I've caught them in the web I stab them and eat them. This is my Right Cultivation. There are Buddhist monks in the World of Law who unfurl long coils of sutra scrolls and intone them to trap and delude the hearts of people. After they've trapped and deluded their prey, these monks greedily devour the offerings they have received. These monks are of my ilk. I am the monk of the Kusha sect of the World of Creatures, and the monks of the Kusha sect in the World of Law are Spiders."[46]

The Praying Mantis was in the middle section of the assembly. He lifted his head and waved his arms as he spoke: "I am born of the damp energy of the soft grass. My wings are short and I am not an

able flier. If I am pursued when I attempt
to escape, I turn and raise my arms in
attack, even though my pursuer might be
far more powerful than me. People have
made me into a metaphor: "Like a mantis
raising its arms to stop the wheel of a passing cart." This is an extreme insult; it
means the height of stupidity. Since I am
dominated by the sideways energy, I know

nothing of my own foolhardiness. There are as well Buddhist monks
of the World of Law who [belong to the Sanron, or Three Treatise,
sect and] organize their teachings into threes, such as the Three Poisons and the Three Worlds of karmic cause and effect, in an attempt to
reach the True Way, but they remain ignorant of the inherent mutual
natures of the True Way. It is impossible to discuss the True Way in
terms of threes. Their attempt to do so in spite of its impossibility is
precisely like a mantis raising its arms to stop the wheel of a passing
cart. So it is that I am the Sanron-sect monk of the World of Creatures,
and the Sanron-sect monk of the World of Law is a Mantis."[47]

The Mole Cricket was pressed to the
earth at the back of the assembly, fast
asleep. The other creatures laughed to see
him so, and he joined in with his own jolly
harping. "I am born of the dry energy in
the earth. I don't get wet even if I run
through water. If I drink water I die. I live

by inhaling the "markless emptiness." There are Buddhist monks of
the World of Law who teach that the characteristics of all elements of

existence are originally empty and markless. They are deluded by Emptiness just as I am sustained by inhaling it, and they are my ilk. I am the monk of the Hosso sect of the World of Creatures, and the monks of the Hosso sect of the World of Law are Mole Crickets."[48]

The Locust was at the west of the assembly. The creatures pressed him for his opinion, and he leapt out with it: "I am born of the fragrance of the rice blossoms. My body is light and I can leap with great speed. By sucking the energy of the rice flowers I harm them. There are Buddhist monks in the World of Law who are just as fond of the flower of the mind. They are of the Kegon sect, and though they fervently contemplate this flower of the mind they do not know that the mind is made up of sentiment and intellect in a mutual relationship. I am born from the rice blossom, yet I harm it. These monks speak of the flower of the mind, yet they are deluded about the mind. So it is that they are of my ilk. I am the Kegon-sect monk of the World of Creatures, and the Kegon-sect monk of the World of Law is a Locust."[49]

The Snail was in an upper seat. The other creatures reproached him: "You don't belong in such an elevated seat!" But he responded: "I am born in the grass of high mountains, as well as in the gardens of human beings. I drink dew and suck air, and I think of nothing else. This is because I am born with just a little of the sideways energy. Among the Buddhist monks of the World of Law there are those whose highest practice is the recollection of the syllable *a*. But they do not know that the faculty of recall is only recall when it exists in its mutual relationship with memory. They are deceived by an unbalanced sideways mind, and they are of my ilk. I am the Tendai monk of the World of Creatures, as I take refuge in the practice of recollection of the letter *a*. The Tendai monk of the World of Law is a Snail."[50]

The Katydid was toward the lower section of the assembly. It came crawling out
to pipe up: "I am born of the metal energy
of Autumn's Rule. I drink dew and eat the
spoiling seeds of grasses. My cry is like
the jangling of a horse's bit because of the
metal energy in me. The Buddhist monks
of the World of Law who [belong to the
Shingon, or True Word, sect and] greedily

eat without cultivating, ringing their bells and shaking their jangling
metal staffs, do so in imitation of me. They deceive the people and
rob them in the name of receiving donations. They make false words
their "True Words." These are of my ilk. I am the Shingon-sect monk
of the World of Creatures, and the Shingon-sect monks of the World
of Law are all Katydids."[51]

The Pine Cricket was on the left side of
the assembly. He crept forward, saying: "I
am born as a result of the response of
metal energy to the essence of the pine
tree. I drink dew and do not eat any
defiled thing. My voice is light, like the
ringing of a tiny bell. Certain Buddhist

monks of the World of Law ring all sorts of bells as they intone the
Buddha's name. They call the little bell they tap when they intone the
Buddha's name with faith a "pine cricket," after me. So it is that they
are of my ilk. I am the Pure Land-sect monk of the World of Creatures,
and the Pure Land-sect monk of the World of Law is a Pine Cricket."

The Cicada was to be found on two sides of the assembly, east and west. The Cicada on the east said: "I am born of a subdivision of the Pine cricket, of the same metal energy that governs autumn. I, too, drink dew. My chest and stomach are hollow, which is why I am able to drone on so long. There are certain Buddhist monks of the World of Law, too, who belong to [the Ikko sect,] a subdivision of the Pure Land sect. They drone the Buddha's name on and on, no different from my droning. I drone on mindlessly, in emptiness, while they drone with a great desire for offerings running sideways through their hearts. With their sideways thoughts and my sideways energy, their intoning and my droning, we are of the same ilk. I am the Ikko-sect monk of the World of Creatures, and the Ikko-sect monk of the World of Law is a Cicada."[52]

The Late Cicada was on the fringe of the assembly, to one side. He wobbled out and spoke: "I am born of a subdivision of other cicadas, and I have the energy of the receding phases of fire and metal in a mutual relationship. When the receding energy in me responds to the energy at the waning period of a season, I alight on this tree and call like a ringing bell, or I flit to that tree and call again. There are Buddhist monks [of the Ji, or Timely, sect] in the World of Law who arrive in one place and sell holy cards, then flit to another place to sell holy cards. They deceive the people and are greedy for donations, and they are of my ilk. So it is that I am the monk of the Ji sect in the World of Creatures, and the monk of the Ji sect in the World of Law is a Late Cicada."

The Daddy Longlegs Spider was at one side of the assembly, hiding under a rush mat. The other creatures inquired of him: "Why do you hide?" After a while, the Daddy Longlegs came out from his hiding place and spoke: "I am born from the energy of hidden dampness in mountain valleys or the crevices of human homes. My legs are long and my body tiny. I huddle together with others of my kind and criticize other creatures. We take great pride in our long legs because our minds are unbalanced due to the sideways energy. There are Buddhist monks in the World of Law [of the Lotus, or Nichiren, sect] who know nothing of the True and Subtle Way but are deluded and unbalanced by certain strange subtleties, and so they preach the Lotus Sutra. Though they are deluded by the Lotus Sutra, they believe in it firmly and are unbalanced by the sideways energy. Soon the entire sect is unbalanced, and they criticize other sects. In this, they are of my ilk. I am the monk of the Lotus sect of the World of Creatures, and the monks of the Lotus sect of the World of Law are Daddy Longlegs."

The Dragonfly was flitting here and there above the assembly as if he were the only one present. The other creatures pressed him for his opinion. And in reply the Dragonfly said: "I am a metamorphosis of an insect of damp ground. My intelligence is elevated; I am so bright that I can see beyond Heaven. Yet I fly sideways, and however free I may think myself, mine is not the freedom of the Living Truth when it flows in the upward direction. There are Buddhist monks in the World of Law [of the Soto Zen sect] who accumulate great merit in their practice and achieve enlightenment, so that they can see beyond Heaven. But though they claim that they are free, they are ignorant of the Subtle Way of the mutual natures of the Living Truth. Their minds are, in fact, dominated by the sideways energy, unbalanced and deluded. They are of my ilk. So it is that I am the Soto Zen monk of the World of Creatures, and the Soto Zen monk of the World of Law is a Dragonfly."[53]

The Butterfly was in the upper part of the assembly to the east. It opened its wings and spoke: "I am born as a transformation of the energy of various flowers. My body is light and I can flit up and down. Just as fire means smoke and smoke means fire, I have attained the extreme of freedom. I drink the dew of flowers, I purify my heart, I gaze at flowers, and I lose myself in appreciation of the scenery until my ability to think is atrophied, all because I am dominated by the sideways energy. There are Buddhist monks [of the Rinzai Zen sect] in the World of Law who compose poems about the Moon, the flowers, the snow, and the beautiful scenery, who allow their spirits to grow atrophied through the exercise of foolish considerations and discriminations, who indulge their emotions, who let their wills grow unbalanced, who are deluded and confused and ignorant of the Subtle Way of the mutual natures of the Living Truth inherent in them. In their sideways intellects and their unbalanced confusion they are of my ilk. So it is that I am the Rinzai-sect monk of the World of Creatures, and the Rinzai-sect monks of the World of Law are Butterflies."[54]

The Bell Cricket came forward from his seat and said: "I am born from the metal energy that governs autumn. I drink dew and do not consume defiled foods. My voice is as pure as a bell. Yet I am governed by the sideways energy and so I am not able to exercise the divine powers of the operation of the upward energy of the Living Truth. There are human beings in the World of Law, too, who [are devotees of Shinto and] ring bells and intone prayers. But they do not know that consciousness is the subtle god, operating in mutual relationships. Since they are unbalanced and deluded by the sideways energy, they are of my

ilk. I am the Shinto priest of the World of Creatures, and the Shinto priests of the World of Law are Bell Crickets."

The Conch was on the outskirts of the assembly, but it crept forward. "I am a metamorphosis of a mountain bird, the Pheasant. When you blow my empty shell after I am dead, it resounds like a horn. The reason it sounds unbalanced and unsteady in tone is that I am a meta-

morphosis of the sideways energy. There are those in the World of Law [called *yamabushi,* or mountain ascetics] who say that the sound of my shell dispels delusion, but those who blow on it sit on the border between Buddhism and Shinto and they are unbalanced and deluded by the sideways energy, just as I am. They are of my ilk, and I am the mountain ascetic of the World of Creatures; they are the Conches of the World of Law."

The Blister Beetle was sitting apart from the rest. Yet he, too, came out to speak. "I am born of the energy of damp fire in the mountain ranges, and I am poisonous. I kill any creature I touch. There are in the World of Law people [known as doctors] who, without any knowledge of the circulation of energy as mutual natures in human bodies or herbs, prescribe medicines based on their own foolish guesses and make a living by murdering people. These are of my ilk. So it is that I am the doctor of the World of Creatures, and the doctors of the World of Law are Blister Beetles."

The Horsefly was in a place toward the lower section of the assembly. He came forward to speak, too: "I am a metamorphosis of insects of damp earth. The damp fire energy rises in me and I cannot see. I fly about guided by odor and with two sharp fangs in my mouth I suck the blood of cattle and horses. There are in the World of Law blind people who walk about with the help of a stick, visiting people's homes and greedily begging for food. They are of my ilk. I am the blind beggar of the World of Creatures, and the blind beggars of the World of Law are Horseflies."

The Crab of the World of Creatures moves in a sideways fashion, and the minds of the people of the World of Law do likewise. In the World of Creatures, the Bagworm hangs from trees, and in the World of Law there are those who do nothing but hang around idling. There are Inchworms in the World of Creatures, and trifling fools in the World of Law. In the World of Creatures we find Slugs; in the World of Law, sluggards. The World of Creatures has its Crickets, and the World of Law has its idiots. There are Dayflies in the World of Creatures, and in the World of Law there are those who die young. There are Silkworms in the World of Creatures, and prisoners in the World of Law. In the World of Creatures there is the Soldier Bug; in the World of Law, the brigand. There are clouds of Mosquitoes in the

World of Creatures and gangs of thieves in the World of Law. In the World of Creatures there are many, many creatures with useless shells; in the World of Law, there are beggars, wandering monks, craftsmen, merchants, actors, male prostitutes, courtesans, and tea-house girls—a multitude of useless occupations. They all exist because of the establishment of laws.

In the World of Creatures, many insects cry and call under the domination of autumn. This is the same as the many different kinds of music-making in the World of Law, song and dance, Noh, the narratives of the puppet theater, the lute, the samisen, and all other musical instruments. The people of the World of Law capture insects and put them in cages to enjoy their calls or to watch the flickering of the Fireflies' light. This does not happen in the World of Creatures, and is sure proof that the evil of the people of the World of Law far exceeds that of the World of Creatures. And even when insects that have been caught and kept in cages are released again to their homes, they weaken and die. They have been destroyed by their contact with the upward energy of human beings. This is a great evil of the human beings of the World of Law, and one that the various creatures lament most grievously.

The assembly of creatures pronounced its verdict: "It is due to the establishment of the World of Law that human beings are lost in lust, in drink, in gambling, in arson and theft. Because there is no end to exploitation and violence among the people of the World of Law, an emperor, a feudal lord, a retainer who is defeated in battle can become a slave or a beggar. A slave or a commoner can rise to be emperor, feudal lord, or retainer. This cannot happen in the World of Creatures, which proves that the human estate is a lowlier one than ours. The people of the World of Law may perish during years of famine, they may be forced to flee under pressure from their debts, they may have to desert their land and wander homeless because they cannot pay their taxes, they may suffer poverty, they may thieve, they may bring ruin to their house through luxury, they may rule others with arrogance and cause uprisings, they may lend money to others and in their greed fret that they do not make enough interest. All of these are products of the World of Law with its lust and thievery, delusion and confusion. In the World of Creatures, we suffer none of these calamities. Our emperor will not suddenly change into a slave, there is no famine in years of bad harvest, there is no lending or borrowing of money, no pains of wealth or poverty, no fleeing or homeless wandering, no one lost in lust or drink. There is no selfish desire at all, no exploitation or revolt. We eat the food provided us by Heaven's Truth, and our Right Cultivation is the hierarchy in which large eats small. Compared to the people of the World of Law, our lives in the World of Creatures are peaceful, with ample food and clothing. Ah, how lamentable. Human beings are born governed by the upward energy and all due to a small error they fall under the governance of the sideways energy and establish the World of Law of unbalanced delusion caused by the sideways energy."

So it was the creatures all assembled and for the people of the World of Law lamented. How admirable indeed!

Since there is no use of gold or silver in the World of Creatures, there is no desire or confusion, thievery or revolt.

GATHER TO DISCUSS THE WORLD OF LAW

The Whale sent out a proclamation, and it was announced throughout the great ocean in all directions, everywhere without exception.

In accord with his command, all the fishes of the seas and rivers assembled. Then it was that the Whale spoke to his gathered subjects: "I have heard that recently the birds, the beasts, and the creatures have each held their own assemblies. Though our kind lives in the seas and we may appear to be different from land animals, all of the four kinds of creatures are alike in that we are all born of the Subtle Way of the mutual natures of Heaven's Truth as it circulates in a sideways manner. Should we fishes fail to discuss the World of Law, we would be opposing the Subtle action of the mutual natures of the four types of creatures, who are all born of the sideways energy and are meant to act in unison. We would be inviting the wrath of Heaven's Truth. So be it: Let each of you discuss the human beings of the World of Law." And all the fishes bowed low.

The Whale continued: "The Whale is the emperor of the World of Fishes. The Dolphin is the aristocrat, the Whale Shark is the generalissimo, the Tuna are the feudal lords, the Sharks are the various officials, the Bonito is the retainer, the Yellowtail is the footsoldier, the Sea Bream is the craftsman, the Sea Bass is the merchant, the Sea

Trout is Shakyamuni, the Salmon are Buddhist monks, the Spanish Mackerel is the wise man, the Barracuda is the Shinto priest, the Flathead is the doctor, the Herring is the mountain ascetic, and all the other small fishes of both oceans and rivers are the beggars, wandering monks, idle folks, and troublemakers. In every case, the larger fish eat smaller fish. I, the Whale, eat Dolphins, Dolphins in turn eat Whale Sharks, Whale Sharks eat Tuna, Tuna eat Sharks, Sharks eat Bonito, Bonito eat Sea Bream, Sea Bream eat Sea Bass, and so on in that order, a hierarchy by which large eats small and small eats yet smaller. Day after day we do nothing but this, for it is the Right Cultivation of the World of Fishes, the lot provided us by Heaven's Truth. The lot provided humans is for all to engage in Right Cultivation and thus create the human world of Living Truth, far superior to our poor World of Fishes. Yet from the time of the appearance of the Sages and Shakyamuni, with their unbalanced delusions caused by the domination of the sideways energy, the World of Law has been established and human beings have become like us, contrary to their birthright and unbalanced by the sideways energy in both thought and deed.

We Whales are born when the vaporized, wet energy of the ocean's salt water condenses into a large mass. This vaporous dampness is sweet. Its sweat condenses into our enormous bodies, which may be as long as one hundred eighty feet. There is no fish that rivals me, and that is why I am the emperor of the World of Fishes. I circle the globe in a single circuit, I look up to Heaven and spout salt water, I dive down to the ocean's depths and observe the veins of oil in the earth's crust.[55] Year after year I swim among my subjects, teaching them, leading them, and ruling the World of Fishes. Since I teach them based on my unbalanced sideways intellect, the thoughts and deeds all my fishes are likewise unbalanced by the sideways energy. The great teachers among the human beings of the World of Law—the great sage-king Fuxi, who created the system of divination; Shennong, who composed the *Classic of Herbal Natural History;* Huang Di, who created the calendar; Yao, who taught the five constant virtues; Shun, who taught music; Yu, who discovered the mysterious floodwater inscriptions; Tang and his writings; Wen, who authored the *Book of Changes;* the Duke of Zhou, who composed classics and odes; and Confucius, Zisi, and Mencius, who each composed many tomes—all of them were of unbalanced intellect, since they were dominated by the sideways energy. They are all of my ilk. So it is that I am the sage-emperor of the World of Fishes, and the sage-emperors and wise and learned men of the World of Law are all Whales."

The Dolphin was in the upper part of the assembly. He spread his fins and spoke: "I am born of the soft vaporous energy of the ocean and I am the aristocrat of the World of Fishes. Should any of you dare to oppose the rule of our lord the emperor, I will capture you and eat you. Among the human beings of the World of Law, too, the emperor consumes the labors of the aristocrats, the aristocrats consume the labors of the generalissimo, the generalissimo consumes the labors of the feudal lords, the feudal lords consume the labors of their officials, the officials consume the labors of their retainers, the retainers consume the labors of the footsoldiers, the footsoldiers consume the labors of the merchants below them, and among commoners, the master consumes the labors of his servants. That hierarchy by which larger eats smaller is exactly like ours in the World of Fishes. Thus it is that just as I receive the commands of our emperor and then rule you as he wishes, among human beings in the World of Law the aristocrats receive the commands of their emperor and direct the generalissimo in his duty. So it is that I am the aristocrat of the World of Fishes, and the aristocrats of the World of Law are Dolphins."

The Whale Shark was in the upper part of the middle section of the assembly. He opened his eyes wide and they glittered as he spoke: "I am born of the metal energy of the vapors of sea salt. I am powerful, and I am the generalissimo of all the World of Fishes. I will capture and devour each, every, and any one of you who should dare to resist my orders. Among human beings of the World of Law there is as well a generalissimo, who holds forceful sway over all the feudal lords. He is of my ilk. So it is that I am the generalissimo of the World of Fishes, and the generalissimo of the World of Fishes is a Whale Shark."

The Tuna was to be found in the lower part of the middle section of the assembly. He spoke up: "I am born of the water energy of the vaporous dampness in the sea. I am black, my body is fat and heavy, and I am the feudal lord of the World of Fishes. I will not hesitate to capture and devour any of my subjects who dare to oppose my rule." All the fish hunched down in fear. "Among the human beings of the World of Law," continued the Tuna, "there are feudal lords who perversely exploit their subjects. They are of my ilk. So it is that I am the feudal lord of the World of Fishes, and the feudal lords of the World of Law are Tuna."

The Shark was to the left of the assembly. He spoke in a bullying tone: "I am born of the energy of gaps in the vapors of the ocean's salt. My skin is rough and I am strong. I am the official of the World of Fishes. There are among the human beings of the World of Law officials as well. They consume the labors of their retainers and they are of my ilk. So it is that I am the official of the World of Fishes, and the officials of the World of Law are Sharks."

The Bonito was at the right of the assembly. Holding his head with his fins, he spoke: "I am born of the energy of the receding phase of the vapors of the ocean's salt. I am meaty and I eat the small fishes below me. Among the human beings of the World of Law there are retainers, who consume the labors of the footsoldiers below them. They are of my ilk. I am the retainer of the World of Fishes, and the retainers of the World of Law are Bonito."

The Yellowtail was in the lower section of the assembly. He pressed himself down as he spoke: "I am born of the receding wood energy in the ocean's salt. I am finely scaled and I am the footsoldier of the World of Fishes. If any of you Sea Bream should dare to oppose my rule, I will capture you and devour you. Among the human beings of the World of Law there are footsoldiers as well. They consume the labors of the commoners below them, the craftsmen and the merchants. This is the behavior of those of my tribe. So it is that I am the footsoldier of the World of Fishes, and the footsoldiers of the World of Law are Yellowtails."

The Sea Bream was toward the left side of the assembly, and he came forward to speak: "I am born of the fire energy of the salt vapors, unbalanced in the sideways direction, in the sea. My scales are brightly colored. I cling near the shore, where I build homes for other fishes. Among human beings of the World of Law, too, there are those whose profession is to contrive things; they do not cultivate. They are of my ilk. So it is that I am the craftsman of the World of Fishes, and the craftsmen of the World of Law are Sea Bream."

The Sea Bass was toward the right side of the assembly, and now he came forward to speak. "I am born under the domination of the receding phase of the metal energy, unbalanced in the sideways direction, in the sea. My scales are white and shiny. My task is to exchange the foodstuffs of the World of Fishes. Among the human beings of the World of Law, too, they exchange food, clothing, utensils, and all things for metal currency, in the name of commerce. So it is that I am the merchant of the World of Fishes, and the merchants of the World of Law are Sea Basses."

The Sea Trout was in a high seat in the upper part of the assembly. He spoke: "I am born of the metal energy as it circulates in a sideways direction in the sea. I swim up rivers and in their fresh water I purify my mind so that it grows unbalanced. I rest in river hollows and there I meditate, again and again. Among the human beings in the World of Law there are those who leave their homes and climb up into the mountains, where they sit in silence, meditating, to purify and unbalance their minds. These are of my ilk. So it is that I am the Buddha of the World of Fishes and the Buddha of the World of Law is a Sea Trout."

The Salmon was just below the Sea Trout in the upper part of the assembly, and he spoke next: "I am born dominated by the advancing phase of the fire energy as it circulates unbalanced in the sideways direction in the sea. I follow the teachings of the Sea Trout and like him climb up rivers. In the river hollows, facing the banks, I silently rest in my meditations. Human beings in the World of Law become Buddhist monks and, in imitation of the Buddha, they sit in silent meditation. These are of my ilk. So it is that I am the Buddhist monk of the World of Fishes, and the Buddhist monks of the World of Law are Salmon."

The Spanish Mackerel was to one side of the assembly. It lifted its mouth to say: "I am born of the soft receding phase of the unbalanced sideways energy in the sea. On sunny days I float on the ocean's surface and gaze in the four directions. I indulge my emotions and glorify my delu-

sion, thinking mine a great intelligence. Among the human beings of the World of Law, too, there are those who float on the surface of study, who indulge their emotions through poetry and literature, and glorify their own delusion. These ones are of my ilk. So it is that I am the literati, the wise and learned man of the World of Fishes, and the literati, the wise and learned ones of the World of Law are Spanish Mackerels."

The Barracuda was in a corner of the upper section of the assembly. He spoke: "I am born of the metal energy above the waves as it circulates in the unbalanced sideways direction in the sea. On my head there is a crest that resembles a court hat, and as I fly above the waves I cry with a ringing sound, like a bell. Among the human beings of the World of Law, too, there are those who wear court hats and trousers and ring bells and intone prayers with the hearts of Barracudas. These are of my ilk. I am the Shinto priest of the World of Fishes, and the Shinto priests of the World of Law are Barracudas."

The Herring was at one side of the assembly, from which he swam forward to speak: "I am born of the energy of the moments between the rising and the ceasing of the waves, as that energy circulates in an unbalanced sideways direction, in the sea. When you think I'm here, I'm there. I am never still, and I am continually lost between here and there. Among the human beings of the World of Law, too, there are those who follow what seems to be Buddhism but is not Buddhism, what seems to be Shinto but is not Shinto. They straddle both religions in confusion. These ones are of my ilk. So it is that I am the mountain ascetic of the World of Fishes, and the mountain ascetics of the World of Law are Herrings."

The Flathead sat on the eastern side of the assembly, facing west. "I am born of the soft retreating phase of the energy of the salt vapor in the sea. I divide up the food and distribute it to each fish. After they eat the food, many of them die of poisoning. There are among the human beings of the World of Law those who are ignorant of the inherent mutual natures of medicinal herbs and of human full and empty organs, yet they dose others with those medicines and make their livings as murderers. These ones are of my ilk. So it is that I am the doctor of the World of Fishes, and the doctors of the World of Law are Flatheads."

The Gurnard was on the northern edge of the assembly, from

where he spoke up: "I am born of the vaporized fire energy in the sea, and the metal energy, which shares mutual natures with fire, is strong in me. My head, my bones, and my fins are hard and stiff and when I become entangled in the seaweeds near the shore, I can't free myself. I am forced to rely on my companions to free me. There are Buddhist monks in the World of Law who practice religious discipline. When their robe catches on something at the side of the road, their practice is to refrain from freeing themselves. They wait for another to pass and free them. These are of my ilk. So it is that I am the monk of the Ritsu sect in the World of Fishes, and the monks of the Ritsu sect in the World of Law are Gurnards."

The Sardine was on the eastern side of the assembly. "I am born of the energy of the damp vapors in the sea. I am oily, and I can illuminate the dark eon of nothingness.[56] There are Buddhist monks in the World of Law who claim that they can illuminate the eons even preceding the eon of nothingness. These are of my ilk. So it is that I am the monk of the Kusha sect of the World of Fishes, and the monks of the Kusha sect of the World of Law are Sardines."

The Codfish was at the farthest corner of the assembly. "I am born from the energy of the clear, cold salt water in the sea. I rest on the ocean's bottom, I swim through the ocean's middle, and I float on the ocean's surface. Yet though I change my place three times, I am still captured by human beings. There are Buddhist monks in the World of Law who preach the Three Teachings. They are of my ilk. So it is that I am the Sanron-sect monk of the World of Fishes, and the Sanron-sect monks of the World of Law are Codfish."

The Gizzard Shad spoke up from the back of the assembly: "I am born of the energy of the central damp fire vapor in the sea. Though I am extremely smelly, inside I am without any attachments, without characteristics. Among the Buddhist monks of the World of Law there are those who claim that the true nature of existence (*hosso*) is without characteristics. They are of my ilk. So it is that I am the Hosso monk of the World of Fishes, and the Hosso monks of the World of Law are Shad."

The Gray Mullet was an the far southern side of the assembly, whence he spoke: "I am born of the energy of the strongly condensed damp vapors in the sea. All my efforts bear fruit. Among the Buddhist monks of the world there are those who call themselves the Jojitsu (fruitbearing) sect, and these are of my ilk. So it is that I am the monk of the Jojitsu sect of the World of Fishes, and the monks of the Jojitsu sect of the World of Law are Gray Mullets."

The Blowfish spoke from outside the assembly. "I am born of condensed vapors from places in the sea where fresh water flows into salt water, and the two are not yet mixed. That is why I am an aggressive, belligerent, and poisonous fish. My skin is covered with white star-shaped spots that resemble a robe patterned with flower garlands (*kegon*). There are Buddhist monks of the World of Law who wear glorious robes and surplices but their minds know nothing of the mutual natures of the Living Truth. They delude the masses and are deadly poisonous. They are of my ilk. So it is that I am the monk of the Kegon sect of the World of Fishes, and the monks of the Kegon sect of the World of Law are Blowfish."

The Saurel was in a northern corner of the assembly. He spoke

up: "I am born of the initiating wood
energy in the sea. My scales are rough as
armor and my fins sharp as swords. At the
slightest instigation I fight with other fish.
Among the Buddhist monks of the World
of Law, too, there are those who at the
slightest instigation don armor and battle

with other monks.[57] They burn the temples of other monks and violate the Buddha's way; they follow a demon's path instead. These
ones are of my ilk. So it is that I am the Tendai monk of the World of
Fishes, and the Tendai monks of the World of Law are Saurels."

The Mackerel spoke as he circled the outskirts of the assembly.
"I am born of an energy with great force, unbalanced in the sideways direction, in the sea. I swim to far distant shores and then
swim back again. I deceive the Whale and eat his blubber, and in
my travels through the seas I deprive other fishes of their food as
well. Among the Buddhist monks of the World of Law there are
those who travel to other countries and then return home. They
deceive the emperor and devour his donations. They also travel
from province to province and devour the donations of the populace. When they have accumulated enough riches, they return to
the laity. Such ones are of my ilk. So it is that I am the Shingon
monk of the World of Fishes, and the Shingon monks of the World
of Law are Mackerels."

The Octopus was on one far side of the assembly. He spoke from
his seat: "I am a metamorphosis of a serpent. I have many arms and
on those many arms many eyes. When I come to an Octopus trap I
crawl in and devote myself to religious practice. I tap the trap with my

arms and say, 'Your birth in the Pure Land has been determined!' Among the Buddhist monks of the World of Law, there are monks of the city who are metamorphoses of mountain hermits. They wander here and there and with deceit-filled eyes they tap on bells and proclaim that their listeners' birth in the Pure Land has been determined. Such ones are of my ilk. They are unbalanced and deluded by the sideways energy. So it is that I am the Pure Land monk of the World of Fishes, and the Pure Land monks of the World of Law are Octopi."

The Squid was sitting in an eastern corner of the assembly. "I am a metamorphosis of the Crow. On sunny days I float in the troughs between the waves, open my mouth, and cry 'Awa, Awa!' in a hundred different voices. I steal the food of Gulls. Among the Buddhist monks of the World of Law, there are those who are a metamorphosis of another sect. They, too, open their mouths and cry, 'Amida, Amida!' in a hundred different voices. Such ones are of my ilk. So it is that I am the Ikko sect monk of the World of Fishes, and the Ikko sect monks of the World of Law are Squids."

The Flatfish was at the bottom of the assembly. He said: "I am born of the energy of the foam of the ocean's salt water. I swim up rivers, stopping here and there, making a print of my fins in one place and then moving on and making another print of my fins in another place, swimming round and about. Among the Buddhist monks of the World of Law, there are those who travel from province to province and place to place, pasting up their holy cards here, deceiving the populace, and then going to another place and pasting their holy cards up there. All the while they rob the people of their donations, which they greedily devour. Such ones are of my ilk. So it is that I am the Ji-sect monk of the World of Fishes, and the Ji-sect monks of the World of Law are Flatfish."

The Striped Mullet was at the southern edge of the assembly. "I am a lake fish. My scales are tough, and I imitate the Carp, who leap up waterfalls. I outpace the Lesser Fishicle and practice the way of the Greater Fishicle.[57] But since I am dominated by the sideways energy, I am not capable of attaining the True Fishicle. Among the Buddhist monks of the World of Law there are aggressive ones with tough determination. They split off from the Tendai sect and formed their own group whose aim is to surpass the Lesser Vehicle and practice the Greater Vehicle. But since they, too, are dominated by the sideways energy they spout strange subtleties and do not approach the True Subtlety. These ones are of my ilk. I am the Lotus-sect monk of the World of Fishes, and the Lotus-sect monks of the World of Law are Striped Mullets."

The Carp was in the upper section of the assembly, to one side. He spoke: "I am the ruler of all lake fishes. My body is pure and agile, my scales are thick, I am superior to all other fishes, and I leap up waterfalls, trying to reach and even surpass Heaven. But because I am dominated by the sideways energy, I cannot reach Heaven, and so I am still the

fish you see before you. Among the Buddhist monks of the World of Law, too, there are those who devote themselves to their practice, transcending the water which is the focus of their concentrations, and trying to stick their heads above Heaven. But since they are unbalanced and deluded by the sideways energy, they cannot apprehend the upward energy of the Living Truth and they are still the deluded, unbalanced ones they always were. So it is that these ones are of my ilk. I am the Zen monk of the World of Fishes, and the Zen monks of the World of Law are Carp."

All of the smaller fishes, from the Crucian Carp on down—the Anchovy, the *Amago*, the Halfbeak, the *Isaza*, the Whitebait, and the little miscellaneous fishes of the rivers and streams such as the Loach, the Dace, the *Gigi*, the Sweet Smelt, the Eel, the Salamander, and the Shrimp—all such little fishes are of the same ilk as the useless idlers of the World of Law, that is, the beggars, the outcasts, the day laborers, the wandering monks, the imitation artists, the actors, the courtesans, and the prostitutes. So it is that the little fishes are the useless idlers of the World of Fishes, and the useless idlers of the World of Law are miscellaneous little fishes.

On sunny days the fishes swim up to the water's surface and leap through the waves, slapping them with their fins in play, just as people in the World of Law sing and dance. They come up to the surface and spread their fins and sing and dance, just as the people of the World of Law practice the chanting and dancing of the Nō theater. The various little fishes gather at night in the river shallows and make their cries and calls, just as the people in the World of Law chant the puppet theater narratives, sing popular tunes, and play the harp, the lute, and the samisen. Fishes gather in pools to sport, just as people of the World of Law lose themselves in lust, in drink, and in gambling. Such are the resemblances of the World of Fishes and the World of Law.

But the human beings of the World of Law capture fish and put them in creels and tubs until they eat them. This is a great crime that is unheard of in the World of Fishes. Fish that have been kept in tubs for several days cannot return to their original way of life, even when set free again. They weaken and die. This is because during the time they were being kept, their sideways energy was destroyed by the upward energy of human beings. In addition, they are unable to pass through the natural cycle of phases and changes when kept in a tub, and so when the time comes for one of those changes they fail to accomplish it and die.

After intense consideration, the Sea Bream spoke out: "As I see it, I have four fins, just as people have arms and legs—in other words, four limbs. But should I wish to stand up like a human being, and, after making a plea to Heaven, actually try to stand like a human being, I will only be able to see for any distance at all in a sideways direction. I will not be able to see Heaven above, or anything in front or in back of me. This would be a terrible inconvenience, and I wouldn't be able to eat. Then I would take back my plea and return to my stance as a fish.

"There are human beings of the World of Law, too, who, though born of the upward energy, wish to stand on top of others, to live a glorious and luxurious life without cultivating. As they plot how to achieve this, their hearts grow rife with ambition and desire and their upward energy grows more and more blocked. Soon their minds fall into chaos and they plot an uprising, undoing themselves and putting themselves to death. Clearly, these human beings are far more foolish than I."

The Fish declared together: "This great assembly of all the fishes without exception is an extremely rare event, never to occur again. Though our world and the human beings' World of Law resemble each other in many ways, in the World of Law the emperor can become a slave and a slave rise to become the emperor. Even a person from another land altogether can become the emperor! The generalissimo can fall to common status and a commoner can become the generalissimo. The feudal lords can become beggars, and beggars can become feudal lords. The master can become a servant and the servant a master. Why is everything in the human World of Law so confused, so indeterminate?"

One fish replied: "Human beings are born under the governance of the upward energy. They are all meant to engage in Right Cultivation, and all distinctions of ruler and ruled, wise and foolish, good and evil, are by nature foreign to their state. Theirs is a world of people of Living Truth, with no discriminations. Yet certain humans were born with natures unbalanced toward purity. They suppressed the upward energy that governed them and roused the sideways energy that naturally lies suppressed below the upward energy until it became their dominating energy. Under the domination of the sideways energy their sentiments became unbalanced, their intellects became unbalanced, they were deluded and confused, and with their selfish minds unbalanced by the sideways energy, they pushed themselves above others and made themselves emperors. They created ruler and ruled and established the World of Law. Thus it is that raising oneself above the people and claiming to rule the land is in fact the source of all thievery and revolt. As the rulers in this fashion thieve Heaven's Way, the ruled begin to steal possessions, and ruler and ruled are linked in an endless cycle of thievery. When thievery is rampant, revolt is bound to occur, and so the World of Law with its thievery and revolt is born. In our world, it is true, there are large and small, ruler and ruled, and the large eat the small as the rule provided us by Heaven's Truth. This is no crime on our parts, it is our inherent lot. All four kinds of living creatures, the birds, the beasts, the creatures, and the fish, are alike in that large eats smaller, smaller eats smaller still, and smaller still eats smallest. Yet all human beings have bodies of nearly the same size. There are no huge or tiny human beings. This is clear proof that all are meant to engage in Right Cultivation, and no other task is provided them. We are able to see this with our own eyes because we do not oppose the lot provided us by Heaven. For human beings, who are born under the governance of the upward energy, to give themselves up to the dominance of the sideways energy is to thieve the lot provided them by Heaven. They are not aware of this because, though they are meant to be governed by the upwards energy, their behavior is that of the sideways energy. Their delusion is far deeper than ours. What a truly pitiable state of affairs!"

Another fish said: "The human beings of the World of Law also have the worries of wealth and poverty. The rulers exert great pains to extract taxes from the ruled, and the ruled worry greatly about paying their annual tribute and harvest taxes. Those who grow wealthy lend their money, and proceed to worry about not having charged sufficient interest. Those who are poor borrow the money, and fear they will be unable to repay it. When the harvest is bad, the poor die of starvation, or are forced to desert their lands, or lose their homes and are forced to live in rented quarters. So many, many delusions, that force the rulers to worry and the ruled to suffer; the rich are stricken and the poor are oppressed. Why is it that no human being is free from such distress and suffering?"

Another fish replied: "This is all because human beings, who are born under the governance of the upward energy, adopt the behavior of the four types of other creatures. We are born governed by the sideways energy and we behave as the sideways energy dictates. We do not thieve Heaven's Way, and so we have no famine in years of bad harvest, we are not forced to pay annual tribute, we do not engage in lending and borrowing, as the wealthy and the poor do, we are not forced to desert our lands or to live in rented homes, we do not know the sufferings of beggars and outcasts. Because human beings, who are born under the governance of the upward energy, suppress their upward energy and thieve the Way of Heaven by acting according to the dictates of the sideways energy, they themselves violate the Way of Heaven and are unable to free themselves from these sufferings and pains. They make their World of Law identical to the worlds of the four types of creatures, where big eats small; and above and beyond that they are never free of these pains and sufferings, so their lot is far worse than ours, and their sin is deep. Yet their Sages proclaim: 'Those who disobey the law are no better than birds, beasts, creatures, and fish.' What a ridiculous utterance, worth less than a fart!"

And all the fishes broke into laughter. For it is indeed true that in the World of Fishes there is no famine, none of the sufferings of being squeezed to pay taxes and tribute, no wealth or poverty, no liv-

ing in borrowed homes. The World of Fishes is a place of great com-
fort and peace, far superior to the World of Law.

Among the four types of living creatures under the governance of
the sideways energy, large eats small, and so small creatures fear
larger ones and larger ones capture and eat smaller. Since the minds
of human beings of the World of Law are unbalanced by the sideways energy as well, they fear those above them, and in their fear
they slander their rulers. They bully and badger those below them.
All are deluded by dreams of self-benefit, just as the four types of creatures. Among True Men born under the governance of the upward
energy, with purity and impurity subtly and equally balanced in them,
there is neither praise nor blame.

The Fish observed the human beings of the World of Law, bound
as they are by all sorts of laws and regulations, and laughed aloud:
"The root of all evils is in the ruler. Trying to control society without
severing this root is not only useless but another crime of the ruler."

*Our look at the worlds of the four types of creatures has not been
out of hatred for the World of Law, but rather out of sadness at the
great difference between the True Way and the self-serving law, and
the great delusion of people in the world governed by it.*

*In the World of Fishes there is no use of gold or silver currency,
and so there is no lust or delusion, no thievery or revolt. How sad
indeed, how regrettable! All because of the use of gold and silver
currency in the human World of Law, there is no end to lust and
delusion, thievery and revolt.*

NOTES

THE BIRDS GATHER TO DISCUSS THE WORLD OF LAW

1. Prince Shotoku (574–622) was regent during the reign of Empress Suiko (r. 593–628). He was known for his brilliant intellect and wide learning, and particularly for his faith in the newly introduced Buddhist religion.

2. From ancient times, the Chinese have regarded the owl as an unfilial bird, since young owls were said to kill both their parents.

3. Shoeki is satirizing the five constant practices of Confucianism: propriety (*li*), humanity (*ren*), righteousness (*yi*), wisdom (*zhi*), and faithfulness (*xin*). The "superior man" refers to the Confucian ideal of the true gentleman.

4. Bodhidharma (?–528?) is a semi-mythical figure, a South Indian monk credited with introducing Chan (Jap., Zen) Buddhism to China.

5. The Lotus Sutra is one of the classics of the movement of Buddhism known as Mahayana, or "the Great Vehicle." In Japan, the Tendai and Nichiren sects were based on the Lotus Sutra.

6. The *Ran* is, like the phoenix, a fabulous bird of ancient China. Resembling a cock, its feathers were red mixed with blue, yellow, white, and black (the "five colors") and it called with the five notes of Chinese music.

7. Shinran (1173–1262) was founder of the True Pure Land sect, an offshoot of the Pure Land sect (see note 9). He taught the recitation of Amida Buddha's name as a sign of gratitude for salvation.

8. Amida (Skt., Amitabha) is a mythical Buddha said to reside in the Western Paradise, to which believers go after death. Amida was the exclusive object of reverence in the Pure Land and True Pure Land sects but he was also worshiped in many other sects of Japanese Buddhism.

9. Honen (1133–1212) was the founder of the Pure Land sect. He taught the single-minded recitation of Amida Buddha's name as a means to salvation and birth in the Pure Land. Honen composed a well-known vow to be born in the Pure Land, which Shoeki refers to here.

10. The *Chin* is a fabulous bird of China, said to be so poisonous that a single feather dropped in wine would render the drink deadly.

11. The *Kiba* is a fabulous bird of Buddhist legend with two human heads on a bird's body.

12. The Six Sects were sects of Chinese Buddhism introduced to Japan during the Nara period as a sort of scholastic curriculum of Buddhist Studies. Although each sect had its headquarters in a particular temple, many monks mastered the teachings of several, or even all, of the sects. For details on the individual sects see notes 44–49.

13. Saicho (767–822) traveled to China, where he studied the Tiantai sect and esoteric Buddhism, returning to China to found the Tendai sect, which dominated Japanese Buddhism for centuries to come. This sect, with headquarters on Mount Hiei, was based on the Lotus Sutra, but it incorporated many other teachings and practices. Kukai (774-835) was a younger contemporary of Saicho who also traveled to China to study the esoteric teachings of Buddhism recently introduced to China from Tibet and India. He founded the Shingon sect with headquarters on Mount Koya. Kukai became a popular cultural hero, and was credited with inventing the Japanese syllabary.

14. In Chinese, the bird of paradise is called the "wind bird," because it was supposed to be flightless except when the wind blew. It was said not to eat food, but to face the wind and open its mouth, as if it were eating the wind.

15. Shoeki parodies the claims of the Nichiren sect of Japanese Buddhism that only its followers will attain enlightenment. Nichiren (1222–82) taught that the Lotus Sutra was the only true Buddhist teaching and he openly criticized the monks and followers of other schools.

16. The Timely, or Ji, sect was founded by Ippen (1239–89). It taught living each day as if it were the last and the exclusive practice of reciting the name of Amida Buddha. On a pilgrimage to Kumano Shrine, Ippen received an oracle telling him to distribute holy cards with the words "Praise to Amida Buddha" on them to all living creatures. The oracle was in the form of a four-line acrostic verse, the first words of each line creating the phrase "six hundred thousand people." Ippen spread his teachings by traveling around the country distributing holy cards with the words "Six Hundred Thousand Believers Born in the Pure Land."

17. According to ancient legend, Izanami and Izanagi were the male and female gods who created Japan and all its other gods through their intercourse. According to the account in the *Nihon Shoki,* Izanami and Izanagi did not know how to copulate until a wagtail lit near them and began bobbing its head and tail.

18. "Inexpressible in words" is a frequently employed description of the ultimate truth of Buddhism.

19. Fuxi is a legendary ruler of ancient China, the first of the Three August Sovereigns. He is credited with having taught humanity to fish, domesticate animals, and to cook food, as well as divination with the trigrams, writing, and music.

20. The brothers Cheng refers to Cheng Mingdao (1032–85) and Cheng Yichuan (1033–1107), two brothers who revived Confucianism.

21. Zhu Xi (1130–1200) was the great Chinese systematizer of Neo-Confucianism. His teachings had a tremendous influence in Korea and Japan as well.

22. Ogyu Sorai (1666–1728) was one of the leading thinkers of the Ancient Learning movement, a reaction from within Japanese Confucianism against the official version of Zhu Xi Confucianism that had been adopted by the government.

THE BEASTS GATHER TO DISCUSS THE WORLD OF LAW

23. Shun was a legendary ruler of ancient China, one of the five sovereigns. Shun wedded two of the daughters of his predecessor Yao, and his bigamy is the target of Shoeki's criticism.

24. According to the *Classic of Herbal Studies*, the *Doku* was a large ape, resembling a gibbon but larger (perhaps it was an orangutan). Supposedly solitary in nature, the *Doku* cried only once and then was silent (*doku* means "solitary," "single," or "once.") It fed on other monkeys, the same source tells us, and it cites the proverb, "A cry of the *Doku* sends all monkeys to flight." Unfortunately the *Wakan Sansai Zue*, the encyclopedia we have taken illustrations from, does not include a picture of the *Doku*. We have taken the liberty of substituting the gibbon.

25. See note 19 for Fuxi. Shennong was the second of the Three August Sovereigns, following Fuxi and followed by Huang Di. Shennong was said to have invented agricultural implements and taught humans to cultivate. He is also credited with first using herbs to prepare drugs and medicines. Huang Di is regarded as the ancestor of the Han Chinese people. He is said to have given them the five grains, introduced weights and measures, and invented the calendar. Yao is the third of the Five Emperors; he was succeeded by Shun (see note 23). The reigns of Yao and Shun were looked to by Confucians as a golden age

of ideal government. Yu (see also notes 33 and 40) was the last of the Five Emperors, and the founder of the Xia dynasty. Instead of choosing his successor from his most able ministers, he was succeeded by his son, and this is regarded as the beginning of dynastic rule. Tang was the founder of the Yin dynasty, which he established by defeating the Xia ruler. Wen was a warrior who prepared the way for the founding of the Zhou dynasty. He is said to have gathered the wise men of the realm around him and governed humanely. Wu was Wen's son and the actual founder of the Zhou dynasty, about the eleventh century B.C. The Duke of Zhou was the younger brother of Wu, and after Wu's death the Duke acted as regent for his brother's heir and ruled wisely. Zisi (?483–?402 B.C.) was a grandson and disciple of Confucius. Mencius (372–285 B.C.) was one of the great thinkers active during the Warring States period, best known for his teaching of the inherent goodness of human beings. Zhouzi refers to Zhou Lianxi (1017–73), the founder of the philosophical school called Song Studies, after the Song dynasty. He was the master of the two Cheng brothers (see note 20). Zhuzi refers to Zhu Xi (see note 21).

26. Liezi was said to be a Taoist active from fifth through fourth century B.C., between Laozi and Zhuangzi. A work bearing that name in eight volumes exists, but doubts have been cast on its authenticity from ancient times. Huainanzi is actually the title of a work of twenty-one chapters by Liu An (?–122 B.C.), the ruler of the kingdom of Huainan in the Former Han dynasty.

27. "Buddha nature" is the capacity within all living things to attain enlightenment. Based on this teaching, the *Hong Zhi Guang Lu* poses the *koan,* "Does a puppy have the Buddha nature—yes or no?"

28. The cat and the fox were both regarded as magical tricksters in Japanese folklore, and they often conspired to deceive humankind.

29. The Japanese word for mouse is *nezumi* and for thief *nusumi.*

30. The badger is another magical beast in Japanese folklore that delights in playing mischief on human beings and was believed to have powers to transform itself into other shapes.

31. In East Asian folklore, foxes were believed to transform themselves into other creatures, including human beings, to lead people astray and sometimes even kill them.

32. The four classes in China and Japan were the gentleman, farmer, artisan,

and merchant. In China, "gentleman" referred to the ruling bureaucratic class, but in Japan it was the warrior class.

33. These were words of advice that Emperor Shun offered his successor Yu when urging him to accept the throne. Shun remarked that the human heart very easily succumbs to evil, and the heart committed to the Way is subtle and hard to be certain of. As a result, one must keep one's heart pure and focused on the path of moderation.

34. The Buddha mind and the mind of sentient beings are alike in that they share the Buddha nature, but different in their level of spiritual attainment. "The unborn and undying" refers to the ultimate truth, which is beyond all causation. The "five periods" were a popular way of categorizing the Buddhist scriptures in China. The other terms are self-explanatory, except the last, which is one of the names of the Buddha, or Tathagata, who has returned from the realm of enlightenment to our world to teach and save us.

35. The "twelve meridians" are one of the fundamental concepts of traditional Chinese medicine. They were circuits along which energy circulated throughout the body.

36. Because the grammars, including word order, of Chinese and Japanese are so different, Japanese reading Chinese writing were required to hop about the Chinese sentence, skipping up and down and, occasionally, reading a word twice. Such words are called "bracketing expressions"; since English word order is quite similar to Chinese, it is impossible to translate illustrations of such Japanese expressions. The word for "monkey" had a secondary meaning of "still" or "furthermore," and it was one of these twice-read bracketing expressions. Shoeki borrows a popular etymology that was current as early as the Song dynasty in China.

37. A water sprite, or *kappa,* is a water creature of Japanese folklore, usually described as having webbed feet and a turtle's shell, with a pointed beak and a dish-like depression on its head that contained water. If this water spilled or dried up, the *kappa* died. In less carnivorous moods, *kappa* were believed to be especially fond of cucumbers.

38. *The Great Compilation (Taiseikyo)* was composed in the late seventeenth century by a Shinto priest and attributed to Prince Shotoku. It was banned soon after its appearance.

39. The six teachings are Confucianism, military strategy, Taoism, medicine, Buddhism, and Shinto.

THE CRAWLING THINGS GATHER TO DISCUSS THE WORLD OF LAW

40. According the Chinese legend, when Yu tamed a flood he discovered an inscription on the shell of a divine turtle revealed by the receding waters. He copied the words, which were known as the floodwater inscription.

41. The *Book of Songs* is the oldest Chinese poetry anthology. It has been regarded as one of the five Confucian classics. Said to have been compiled and edited by Confucius, it is a collection of folk songs from the Spring and Autumn Annals period through the fifth century. Shoeki mistakenly believed that the Duke of Zhou compiled the *Book of Songs*.

42. *The Doctrine of the Mean* (*Zhong Yong*) is one of the "four books" of Confucianism. It is said to be the composition of Confucius's disciple Zisi and it teaches the unification of Heaven and humanity, advocating the Mean—a doctrine of moderation and balance—as the highest virtue. Shoeki criticizes this concept of a "mean" as dualistic.

43. According to Shoeki, the "eight gates" or sensory organs of the face are the eyeball and the eyelid, the lips and the tongue, the nose and the teeth, and the outer ear and the ear hole.

44. The Ritsu sect is a sect focused on the rules of Buddhist self-discipline, the *vinaya* or, in Japanese, *ritsu*. It is one of the six Nara sects, though it also experienced a popular phase later in the thirteenth century. Because monks and nuns of the Ritsu sect observed the numerous rules of discipline, their way of life was highly restricted.

45. The Jojitsu sect is another of the six Nara sects. It is based on Harivarman's *Jojitsu Ron*. It was more a subject of study than a sect, and was actually studied in conjunction with the Sanron sect (see note 47).

46. Another Nara sect, the Kusha sect is based on the study of the *Abhidharmakosa*, an encyclopedic Theravada text that classifies existence into its components. Like the Jojitsu sect, this is actually a specialized area of Buddhist studies pursued in conjunction with the Hosso sect (see note 48).

47. The Sanron, or Three Treatise, sect was a Nara sect based on two treatises by the Indian Buddhist Nagarjuna and one by his disciple Aryadeva. Its most important teaching, which Shoeki criticizes, is the three truths of the ultimate, the provisional, and the empty. The Three Poisons are common to all Buddhism: greed, hate, and foolishness. So are the Three Worlds, of past, present, and future. The Sanron sect represents one of the two mainstreams of Mahayana Buddhist thought and was very important in the formation of Buddhism, but remained for the most part an academic discipline in Japan.

48. The Hosso, or "Characteristics of the Dharma," sect is an offshoot of the second mainstream of Mahayana philosophy, the Mind-only school. It teaches that all existence was "mind only," and the apparent characteristics of being were essentially empty of an unchanging core. It was introduced to Japan in 653 and is one of the six Nara sects.

49. The Kegon sect is the Japanese version of the Huayan, or Flower Garland, school of Buddhism based on the Avatamsaka Sutra. It was transmitted to Japan in 736 and teaches the interpenetration of each single existing thing with the totality of the universe. Though as one of the six Nara sects it was mostly an academic subject, it had a wide influence on Japanese thought and culture.

50. The Tendai sect was founded by Saicho (see note 13). It is based on the Lotus Sutra but from its inception in Japan included many practices of esoteric Buddhism, including meditation on mantra syllables such as a, the first letter in the Sanskrit alphabet, representing the beginning of all things.

51. The Shingon sect was founded in Japan by Kukai (see note 13). It teaches enlightenment as the integration of man and the cosmos through meditative visualization, recitation of mantras—"True Words," or shingon in Japanese—and the ritual hand positions called mudras. As a sect of esoteric Buddhism, Shingon was characterized by colorful and impressive rites.

52. The Ikko sect is another name for the True Pure Land sect (see note 7).

53. The Soto subsect of Zen was founded in Japan by Dogen. It emphasizes "just sitting" in meditation and strict self-discipline. This was probably the sect that Shoeki entered.

54. The Rinzai subsect of Zen was transmitted to Japan by Eisai in 1168 and again in 1187. It emphasizes attaining enlightenment by wrestling with the mental-spiritual exercises called koan in one-to-one sessions with a Zen master.

THE FISHES GATHER TO DISCUSS THE WORLD OF LAW

55. This line is a parody on a passage from the *Book of Changes*, "Looking up to observe the constellations, looking down to observe the features of the Earth."

56. Buddhist cosmology recognizes four eons, the eon of nothingness, the eon of creation, the eon of sustaining, and the eon of destruction.

57. Shoeki is referring to the practice, especially in the eleventh and twelfth centuries, of monastery complexes such as the Tendai center on Mount Hiei retaining large armies of soldier-monks called *sohei*, who regularly battled with rival temples and the secular authorities.

58. Shoeki's pun is on the Lesser Vehicle (Hinayana) and Greater Vehicle (Mahayana) of Buddhism.

25

The "weathermark" identifies this book as a production of Weatherhill, Inc., publishers of fine books on Asia and the Pacific. Typography, book and cover design: Liz Trovato. Production supervision: Bill Rose. Typesetting: G & H Soho, Ltd., Hoboken, New Jersey. Printing and binding: Arcata/Halliday Litho, Plympton, Massachusetts. The typefaces used are Brighton for text; Della Robia for display.